DREAMS, LOVE, AND MUSIC

LIFESTYLE REVISED

Instagram: www.instagram.com/TheContinent
Twitter: www.Twitter.com/AsiahMillion
Facebook: www.facebook.com/AsiahTheContinent
Spotify: Asiah The Continent
Website: www.AsiahTheContinent.com

DREAMS, LOVE, AND MUSIC

LIFESTYLE REVISED

The Soundtrack of My Life

ASIAH MILLION

DREAMS, LOVE, AND MUSIC LIFESTYLE REVISED
THE SOUNDTRACK OF MY LIFE

Scripture quotations marked KJV are from the Holy Bible, King James Version (Authorized Version). First published in 1611. Quoted from the KJV Classic Reference Bible, Copyright © 1983 by The Zondervan Corporation.

iUniverse books may be ordered through booksellers or by contacting:

iUniverse
1663 Liberty Drive
Bloomington, IN 47403
www.iuniverse.com
844-349-9409

Because of the dynamic nature of the Internet, any web addresses or links contained in this book may have changed since publication and may no longer be valid. The views expressed in this work are solely those of the author and do not necessarily reflect the views of the publisher, and the publisher hereby disclaims any responsibility for them.

Any people depicted in stock imagery provided by Getty Images are models, and such images are being used for illustrative purposes only. Certain stock imagery © Getty Images.

ISBN: 978-1-6632-0760-9 (sc)
ISBN: 978-1-6632-0761-6 (hc)
ISBN: 978-1-6632-0759-3 (e)

Library of Congress Control Number: 2020915944

Print information available on the last page.

iUniverse rev. date: 09/03/2020

CONTENTS

CHAPTER 1

HERSTORY

Once the perception of what I had with him had been broken, I began to see things for what they were and no longer the potential. We were four years into our relationship and not one trace of another woman. No phone calls, no unannounced visits, no hidden panties in his drawers, never responded to his Instagram DMs and likes, nothing! He didn't even turn his head with wandering eyes while we were out together in public on dates. I saw him in ways I had seen no other man.

I've dated men in different parts of the world. No matter how strong the connection, how good the sex, how intense or attached the emotions or how authentic the companionship, there were always other women in the picture. Whether he was just flirting or involved in some kind of relationship, I've always had competition! This had become the norm for me with men in general, but after four years with this guy, I saw him like I saw no other: humble, egoless, honest, loyal, and "the one"!

One morning, while cleaning the house, I picked his jacket up from the back of a chair in the dining room. As I walked toward the closet to hang it up, I heard what sounded like a bunch of Tic Tacs coming from his right pocket. Usually I have to clean his pockets out before doing laundry or putting his clothes away because he's such a big baby. Excited to nibble on something sweet, I put my hand in his pocket, only to pull out a bottle of pills. The label was ripped off, so with honest intentions, I brought the pills to him and asked, "What are these?"

He had just woken up but was still laid out on the bed, stretching and yawning. "Oh, those are just penicillin pills. While traveling, we all got sick on the road. Touring from one event to the next, city to city, state to state, early morning flights out—it's very tiring and so easy to get sick. But I feel much better now."

The lifestyle of dating a celebrity was now making its presence felt. I looked at him with curious eyes. "Then why is the label ripped off?"

After giving me a blank stare for about fifteen seconds, he said, "I don't know, but I feel better, so they're working."

Holding up the bottle of pills, I said, "I'm going to take these to my doctor just to check and see what they are. It's really dangerous going around taking medication that has no label on it."

"There was a label on it," he said in a hostile voice. "It just fell off." He rose from the bed, standing strong in tone and in confidence.

After going back and forth with the guy I saw as "the one," who was trying to convince me that taking the bottle to my doctor didn't make any sense and was a waste of my time, I decided to go anyway.

One thing I did not do was go through my man's phone. If I wanted questions answered, I prayed about it. In dealing with a man with this type of lifestyle, I needed coverage. I kept a relationship with a higher power I had known from my youth: God. Whenever anything seemed unclear, I would always take time out for myself.

Praying was the first part: talking to God, thanking Him, being honest, and asking for what I needed in order to live my purpose. I asked for the strength to deal with answers when they were not the answers I wanted to hear. But meditating was the next part. Many people pray (meaning talk to God), but not many people actually meditate (meaning listen to hear what God is trying to tell them). I had learned from a young age that paying attention served me better than seeking attention. I was ready for answers. That was the only way I could determine my next move.

It was about six o'clock in the morning when my phone rang. An unfamiliar number with not-so-good timing kept me from answering. When the same number popped up on my screen around noon, I decided to take the call.

It turned out to be somebody I used to know—an artist I had worked with many years ago. She had fallen off the face of the earth, and I hadn't heard from her since our last session over a decade ago.

She'd called because she was working on a soundtrack and wanted to bring me in as the main writer and vocal producer. We set a date for a session at the Quad Studio to begin recording. I set it up so that I would be there an hour earlier than her, giving me a chance to vibe with the producer, listen to the tracks she had chosen, and choose the tracks I loved.

As I sat on the couch listening to the tracks, I came up with a few melody ideas. I asked the engineer to set me up in the vocal booth, making sure the mic was the right height and the headphones were plugged in correctly so that I could lay down a reference of my idea. When possible, I like to take my sessions to a spiritual level. I set up the studio in a way that brings me deep into my element: limited company, candles and dim lights in the recording booth, and burning sage on the outside of the booth.

The tracks were eclectic, and the mic and the headphones were crystal clear. It was easy for me to record. I wasn't quite sure what she was feeling for the theme of her soundtrack or where she was in her life, so I didn't create conceptually. I just began to vibe for melody ideas.

While I was in the booth laying down my idea, the music suddenly stopped. I stood there patiently as I watched the engineer get a clean mix of the vocals I'd just laid down. I like to hear the blends of my vocals being mixed as we create, because it allows me to hear translucently, which in turn allows me to come up with more ideas. This is as opposed to recording everything first and then the engineer mixes my vocals once I'm done. If the vocals are dry and unleveled, it deafens me, keeping me from hearing ideas and stifling my creative imagination.

A good engineer knows that a nice mix in your ears as you record will keep you awake and excited to vibe, so I waited patiently. As I waited, I heard a voice. It wasn't coming from either one of the ears of my headphones, so I took off the headphones to listen.

She hit every single note precisely. Her tone fluctuated effortlessly between falsetto and full voice. Her riffs were on point. She wasn't singing super-loud or with consistent power. It was combined with a very chill and sultry tone. The voice seemed to be getting closer and closer, and then suddenly the door to the vocal booth opened.

She peeked in with a smile, and we fell right into each other's arms and hugged. Just when I thought we were finished hugging, she hugged me tighter while apologizing for not being in touch for so long. Then suddenly, she broke into tears.

She had wanted to reach out to me for many years but didn't quite know if it was okay to share what she was going through. She didn't think anyone would even be able to fathom how or why she went through what she went through, but as she explained it, she herself was trying to figure out the purpose of the hurtful experience. I could see that she would need to release whatever she was holding on to before we could begin recording.

Right there on the floor of the vocal booth, we sat and interfaced. I allowed her to vent. The more she spoke, the more pain I felt. The emotion she displayed is what really struck me. She had never been the type to express emotion. She would usually come to the studio ready to sing, with no signs of issues, no drama, no talk-show shit, no sad love songs, no personal stories—just a beautiful voice driven to sing.

I began to get goose bumps—not only because I could relate, but because this was straight déjà vu. She was a young artist who I used to know, now grown. Woman-to-woman, I could see she was ready to explode. So I listened to her story.

As tears rolled down her eyes, creative juices dripped down my soul. Relationship issues held her hostage. She loved the fact that I stayed in my creative lane even while she cried. She felt my love as the pen smoothly recorded her words in blue ink, with wet teardrops between the lines. We both knew this was what we needed in order to do what we'd come to do. I am a woman who thrives off of relationships. Not only did I listen to her for her, but I listened to her for me as well.

Jumping out of a partially rolling taxi, I was amped with anxiety. Somehow, I managed to slip past the registration procedure at the front desk of my gynecologist's office.

"Dr. Freeman, I apologize, but I need your help," I said. "I found these pills in my man's coat pocket, unlabeled. Can you please tell me what these are? He told me they were penicillin, but I—"

"Let me see that," she said as she looked at me with eyes so strong, they felt like they were piercing through mine. Woman-to-woman, it was on like a song.

And the investigation began. She looked at the number on the pill, pulled out a thick book, flipped a few pages, looked up with sorrow, and said, "These are doxycycline. We use these pills to treat STDs, such as chlamydia and gonorrhea."

I couldn't even hear what else Dr. Freeman was trying to say as I walked away in tears. I went back out to the front desk to make an appointment, because now I knew I needed to get myself tested.

After a whole week of going back and forth with this guy I saw as "the one," giving him the opportunity to be honest, he still stood strong.

"I didn't cheat on you," he insisted, "and when your doctor tells you that you don't have anything, make sure you come back and apologize to me. I had no idea these were doxycycline. They

were given to me on the road, along with others who were sick. My manager told me they were penicillin." That was his story, and he was sticking to it.

Finally, I get the phone call I'd been waiting for. The doctor needed me to come in for my test results. That was the longest trip to my gynecologist's office ever. A fifteen-minute ride felt like a whole movie.

"You have tested positive for chlamydia," she said. "Today I'm going to give you a shot and some pills you need to take for ten days."

"Wait a minute, doctor," I interrupted. "I don't have an STD. I thought I might have, but he promised me that he wasn't with anyone else, so perhaps you have the wrong chart. Please check the spelling of my name ..."

"Yes, I know who you are, and this is the correct chart," the doctor replied. "You have chlamydia."

"Wow, God," was all I could think of. Had I believed him, I would never have known that I had an STD.

Furious, I called his phone.

"Hello?" he answered curiously.

"I have chlamydia," I said.

"I'm sorry, baby," he replied. "I'm so sorry. I didn't have sex with anyone. After the show that night, a female got past security and came knocking on my door. She gave me head, but we didn't have sex. I promise."

My ears hurt, but my heart hurt more. I had to hang up. I didn't even care to hear what he had to say after I had given him ample time to be honest. I wanted the honesty. I would have respected him more had he just told the truth, but not only did he lie, he brought something home that love would've never invited. He tried to cure himself and infected me. He had no intention of making sure I got the treatment necessary for myself, which could've had us passing it back and forth, reinfecting each other.

The ride home was worse than the movie I played in my head on the way there. The tears, the rain, the hurt, the pain and the truth ... I had to figure out my next move.

Once I began to analyze our relationship, I knew it was over. I stayed a few weeks in the Hamptons and got in some me time. Lots of tears were shed, but I got some peace of mind. I returned with a more realistic perception.

He apologized profusely, and I did forgive him, but of course I didn't see him the same. He was no longer "the one." I now saw him just as he was: ordinary, basic, and someone who would prevent me from becoming a greater being because he distracted me and broke me down from my come-up.

As I sat with my pen ink bleeding on loose sheets, listening to her story, I began to remember times in the past when I'd see her and she seemed standoffish. I stared into her eyes, replaying the facial expressions she used to wear, trying to make it all make sense.

Breaking down that brick wall of blurred lines was literally a construction job. It was time to rebuild a whole new world of dreams. She wasn't in love with him. She was in love with his potential, who she was hoping he'd become. Her reality was a nightmare, but her faith led her to go live by way of her dreams.

Caught up between the pain he inflicted and the happy place where she came to work, the tears continued to roll down her face. Finally, she said, "Excuse me if I get a little personal, but I have to share this information. I don't mind if you use my story for a song or your book, but this is my story, and it's true."

On a regular day, he knew how I like it—nice slow grinds and deep penetration. When he came home from traveling, being on the road, his sex was different. He was a heavy banger. I could tell when he'd been with other women because the sex strokes were different— feelingless humps and purposeless pumps! Massively numb strokes just to release, not only sexually but emotionally dumping his pain

and gripes with the world all over me, the same way he did his fans and groupies.

It always took him a couple of days to come down and reconnect on a more intimate and spiritual level again. The chaotic energies of offbeat spirits from other women could be felt. Sometimes I would just shake my head and pray over him while he was on top of me, handling his business.

My feelings and needs were always tossed to the side to make sure he was good. His feelings and needs were always upfront and more significant than mine, so this relationship was a win-win situation for him. I always held him down. I forgave him when he cheated, and I understood his weaknesses and sacrificed my own feelings to support his dreams. I always had his back. The problem was, he wasn't able to have mine!

Clearly, I hadn't been pursuing my music, because my part-time gig had become my full-time relationship! I was at a point where I realized I wasn't receiving the support from him that I needed. I wanted to get back into my music career full time, but for the last few years, I felt lifeless and drained. This is my first time back in the studio, because I have gotten life all over again. I'm ready!

I was taking in everything and getting chills, because I knew how she felt. You can be with someone who totally drains you and then be with someone else who lights your soul on fire. After sexually connecting with someone who takes life and then being with someone who gives life, you feel the difference. You recognize that you were slowly dying when you've suddenly come alive.

I listen to artists I work with, especially when I have to write a song for them. I like to tailor the song to their life and make it real. Although time was of the essence, and we were still on studio time, I allowed myself to be there for her emotionally and continue to listen. This would be the most effective part of today's session.

Writing and recording a song without this part is like having sex with no foreplay. It can be done, although it may be a little dry. I knew this was a story that many women would be able to relate to, so as she spoke, my creative juices continued to flow. In an ingenious way, we were actually working.

She went on to say that she had met a guy who'd changed her life. She didn't classify him as husband material, because she was able to identify the category in which he truly belonged. She strongly felt his purpose was to teach her about a few things about herself.

He replenished and put back into her all of the things that had been drained from her previously. The sex was so fulfilling that she didn't need anything more from him. She realized that she'd lost herself in her last relationship because she found herself in this one.

On his California bed, as I situated myself and began to ride, moving to the rhythm of the music that was blasting, he tapped me on the shoulder and whispered in my ear, "Hold on a minute." He went to go turn the music down, way down, where you could barely hear it, and then he lightly spoke: "I'd rather hear your voice."

I began to ride again, and he gently grabbed my head, suggesting that I should look at him. Again, he said, "Hold on a minute." His eyes penetrated mine as he took a peek into my soul. He then said, "Stop fucking me!"

Curiously, I said, "Do you not like it?"

He said, "You don't feel anything!"

I said, "Don't worry about me. I just want to give you something you can feel."

He smiled, rubbed my nose with his, and gently glazed the side of my face, continuing with his nose, and said, "I don't think you understand. I'm not going to get mine if you don't get yours."

Sweat dripping, pudenda throbbing, body shivering, and my mind in a state of euphoria, I surrendered to him. At this point, I knew he knew what he was doing. I gave him full control.

He put his mouth to my ear and asked, "Do you feel this?" while he grabbed my shoulders to pull me down further on top of him. "Do you feel this?" he asked.

"Yes," I said. "That hurts."

He then said, "It only hurts because that's your cervix." He released and then gently pulled me back onto him, grinding with light pressure. Again he asked, "Do you feel that?"

I said, "Yes. Oh my goodness, I have to use the bathroom. I'll be right back."

He then said, "No you don't!" Tugging me gently back toward him, he said, "That's your bladder," as he wrapped his arms around me with the hug of a teddy-grizzly bear—strong but passionately soft. "I want you to relax and feel what I'm about to do next."

Slow but deep grinds, sensual movements, as he pulled me down deeper on top of him. Baritone moans, grizzly grinds, and wet kisses leaving a trail all the way from my neck to my lips. He put his mouth to my ear again and said, "Do you feel this?"

As I began to contract and moan with joy, I said, "Yes, YES," screaming, "I feel it. This feels so good."

He then said, "That's right, because that's your g-spot."

He said he could tell that I was used to being the pleaser, because I struggled with him trying to please me. What does that say about the woman I'd become because of the last man I was fucking? He never even met my ex, but he told me my ex was selfish because he let me take care of him without making sure I was being taken care of.

Dead silence. The feeling of life being put back into her after being with someone who had sucked it all out of her—that was a song from the soundtrack of my life. Her story was so familiar. I told her to get in the recording booth quickly, because that was the level of emotion and passion I was searching for. But equally important, we had a story to tell! We began to vibe creatively, write, and record songs for her soundtrack.

CHAPTER 2

DRIVEN

Speeding on the Long Island Expressway at four o'clock in the morning in my Blue Infinity G35 sports coupe, I was blasting the song I had just finished recording. I was coming from an all-day studio session in Manhattan, about a twenty-three minute drive from Fresh Meadows, Queens, New York, where I lived at that time.

As soon as I got off on my exit, the red light caught me. Five minutes away from home, I was trying to keep my head up from falling. Long days and short nights had become the norm for me for the past few months, so sleeplessness had become an honorable friend of mine. Therefore, it was super-challenging for me to stay awake.

There were no other cars on the road. I looked both ways multiple times before I realized, *If I sit here any longer and wait for cars that are not even coming, I am going to crash.*

To hold my head up from nodding, keep my eyes open from shutting, and maintain my level of consciousness felt like too many tasks to juggle, so I decided to run the light. I follow traffic rules for the most part, but why should I have to sit at a traffic light at four something in the morning when there is no traffic on the road whatsoever? If I thought about what was safe for me, running the red light to keep myself from falling asleep would be safer than sitting at the traffic light at that particular time.

Along with anything amazing that was created, there will be boundaries. I'm not promoting running red lights. Traffic rules were made for a reason. I am simply suggesting that just like traffic rules were made, you have to set boundaries for yourself. You were created by the Creator with your own purpose.

Self-government is the gateway between the rules and your destiny. Once the rules of the game are mastered and we have a level of control over ourselves, our common sense begins to kick in. If we know what gives us drive, we should be able to identify what can cause us to crash.

Your intuition exists within you. It's there to point you in the direction of your purpose. When you ignore your intuition, you're giving the detractor the opportunity to distract you from the signs that could keep you from losing yourself. Sometimes we get so focused on the rules that we tend to make light of what our own bodies are trying to signal to us. We need to give ourselves more credit and allow ourselves to feel what's happening inside us.

We come into contact with so many different people who have so many different ways of life when it comes to culture, religion, and society. We tend to take on their teachings, many times neglecting our own direct impulse, which can bring us to a totally opposite place than being driven: stuck, with no gas. This is one of the biggest reasons we become resentful, mentally ill, lost, harmful to others, and even suicidal. If you feel small, nonexistent, useless, or like you don't have a voice, you begin to think, "What's the purpose of me being here?"

A strong spirit transcends rules. Although we're given rules to follow—at home, at work, at church, on the road, and in relationships—as we evolve and come into our own beings, it is our responsibility to acknowledge and politely avoid what distracts us from our true purpose for being here on earth.

The people around us will always try to control us and have us mastering their rules, but we ourselves should practice self-mastery and embrace who we become as our vision grows clearer, our destination becomes more intentional, and we become more aware of what we're made of and in control of the magic we hold within. It puts us on the starting line, hands us our batons, and equips us with the tools we need in order to beat the rat race. We have the power to create our own lanes. Once we drive in the direction of our calling, we become more aligned with who we were born to be.

Quite often, we are unhappy because we're distracted by things that are going on in the world. The heart wants to be true, but the brain was taught to go against the truth and follow the rules. Your body is literally at war with itself when you don't tend to your truth. It is your responsibility to tap into your inner self and get in touch with your truest being.

As a little girl, I had an involuntary vision that constantly played in my head while awake; that's how I can best describe it. As far back as I can remember, my dreams occurred first thing in the morning when I woke up. I dreaded when it was time to go to sleep. I didn't want to miss out on my day-dreams. My dreams were so vivid that I consciously dodged sleep. I stayed woke!

I've always had the ability to see the bigger picture—the kind of twenty-twenty vision that has visual eyes, allowing me to visualize. I knew I had a purpose. I wasn't sure exactly what my purpose was, but I lived every day trying to figure it out. I was always on a mission and was very sensitive to energies that distracted me from pursuing my dreams. My dreams were my dreams, and I always wanted to know their purpose, because I always felt like there was a reason for everything. That's what gave me life.

When any of my friends would call me sharing their feelings, complaints, or descriptions of unfortunate events taking place in their lives, I would listen. I specifically wanted to find out if they'd talk about something they passionately loved or dreamed about. I wanted to know what would make them happy and how I could help them find the key to their ignition.

Once I know what you're passionate about and you know what I'm passionate about, I can see collaboration possibilities. How can we help each other get the best out of life? However, if we're speaking and throughout the duration of our conversation I hear you complain, my protective instinct starts to kick in. I'll automatically stop what I'm doing and say, "I'm on my way."

Many times, the other person had no idea I was going through my own series of stuff. I didn't verbalize everything I was going through all the time because I just wanted to help fix it. I figured, if I come into your lane to help you out with whatever you're going through, I can get back into my lane once you're back on track, and then we can continue our journey and ride together.

Just as you have to keep your eyes on the road and focus on what's ahead and where you're going, it's equally important to enjoy the journey. It used to affect me when I had to drive past other vehicles I'd see in my peripheral vision, because I'm very sensitive to the energies around me. I never like to compete, because I actually feel bad leaving others behind. I can tell when they're feeling a type of way, so I try to give some level of acknowledgement in passing. But after crashing a few times, I've learned through experience that no matter how badly I want to admire the scenery while en route, it could sabotage my drive.

Without the vision of where you want to go in life, what is your focus? After all, having a destiny to focus on is what keeps us driven. Relationships occur naturally when we come across others on a relatable ship sailing in a relatable direction.

If I'm cruising in the deep blue sea and see someone swimming in the direction I'm headed, I'll offer them a sail on my ship. If they're cruising and I'm the one swimming in the sea, I would appreciate it if they offered me a seat on their boat. I would also do what I could to reciprocate.

Now, if we're both cruising in our own ships and notice each other sailing in the same ocean, and then the waves begin to rise or we see an iceberg ahead, my mindset is, "How can we help each other get to the shore safely?" Others are so focused on their own destiny that they poke holes in your boat or just watch your shipwreck because they want to be the only ship sailing.

Sometimes our current situations keep our mental process from flowing, and we feel stuck. Because I understand that, I try to add value to others by igniting their consciousness. People pay thousands and thousands of dollars to learn and develop themselves educationally but don't make that same investment in learning and growing spiritually. We just don't take enough time out to understand how life truly works. We don't have to settle for the life handed to us. We can have the life we actually desire—but we have to put in our time doing the work that it takes to make the change.

In an unselfish way, I've always wanted everyone to feel what I'm feeling. I want to transfer into the universe that strong spirit that transcends all of the rules and distracts me from becoming better than the things that keep me depressed.

Way before I thought of pursuing my singing career, when I was still living at home with my parents and going to church, I made friends subconsciously with others who could sing, who shared the same craft, and so we ended up on the same journey. Singing always connected me to others, creating a level of fellowship where even outside of church, when we got together, we would sing and dream our feelings out loud in harmony.

One particular friend of mine lived in an apartment building that had the most enticing acoustics. Every time we got on the elevator or took the staircase after a long day of hustling and trying to figure out our next move, listening to our voices blend in her building was something refreshing I'd look forward to. In her Queens apartment one day, while we were singing out loud and exploring different sectional harmony parts, somehow, the focus shifted. We ended up venting about what we were going through in our personal situations with our families. We talked, we cried, we wished for a better life, we laughed, we ordered Domino's pizza, and we sang again until the pizza arrived.

When we got the call that the pizza was here, I jumped up excited to go downstairs. I knew my excitement may have come from a different place than theirs—because one of my issues at home growing up was we didn't know where our next meal was coming from. With so many brothers, sisters, and extended family, food never lasted. Food had become an official solution to many of my problems. As long as I was eating and so was everyone around me, I was happy.

Two out of three of us went downstairs to get the pizza. Smelling the pizza on the elevator ride back up to the tenth floor was almost torture. I wanted to dig in immediately. We walked back into the apartment, put the pizza on the table, grabbed some plates and napkins, and then noticed that the friend who had stayed upstairs was still sitting on the couch. She didn't seem half as excited about the pizza as we were.

I looked at her, slouched over on the couch, and asked her what was wrong.

"I didn't take them all. Don't worry," she said.

I looked at her and asked, "What are you talking about?"

She replied, "The charcoal pills that I took. They're not going to hurt me. I just took them so that I could feel better, and I kept taking more because I wanted to keep feeling better, but I'm fine. I promise. Just go eat."

We ran over to her to see exactly what was going on. Her eyes were heavy; she could barely hold her head up. She looked at us and said, "I'm fine. I didn't swallow all of the pills, look! I have some left." Opening her hands, she showed us seven pills. There were no more pills left in the bottle, and thirty pills was written on the label as the quantity.

Unsure of how many pills were in the bottle at the start of that situation, we immediately tried to make her stand up to see if she was okay. The friend who came downstairs with me ran into the living room with a glass of water. "Here, drink this!" she ordered.

"I'm not drinking any of that nasty water," said our friend who had taken the pills. "Leave me alone." She added, "I'll be fine. Don't worry about me." Then she fell over, unable to stand on her own.

As I put my hand out for my friend who got the water to pass it over to me so that I could continue to convince my other friend to take at least a sip, I noticed she was no longer next me.

"I swear I'm going to jump if you don't drink that water!" came a voice from outside.

Wait, what? I thought. I looked up to see the same friend who came downstairs with me outside on the terrace. She had run outside and was threatening to jump off the terrace if our pill-taking friend didn't drink the water.

"You think you're the only one with issues?" the friend on the terrace yelled. "I got issues too. You think I want to be here? I don't really have anything to live for anyway. Life sucks, my family treats me like shit—so since you want to act up, I will act up too. Shit! I really wouldn't mind dying."

Now I'm inside trying to make friend A on the couch drink some water because of pills she just swallowed, and friend B is outside on the terrace threatening to jump from the tenth floor. I felt like I was caught between a rock and a hard place—trying to get the one on the terrace to come back inside without having to go outside because I was scared of heights.

There I was in the middle trying to balance the two. I didn't want to leave the one on the couch because I was trying to keep her conscious, but I didn't want to disregard the one on the terrace because she could easily fall, even if she changed her mind about jumping voluntarily.

On top of that, I had my own issues. I'd often leave my house to go to the park across the street from where I lived with thoughts of suicide. How did I get here, trying to save two of my friends when I needed help myself? No one ever came to my rescue when I thought about running onto the highway to end my life. They didn't come to my rescue because they didn't even know how bad my situation was and what was on my mind. I never indicated that it was that bad for me. I wanted to know for myself if this was what I truly wanted, and I wasn't looking for that kind of attention. I also realized that I wasn't looking to die. I was looking for *life*.

Maybe God gave me those suicidal thoughts just so that I could empathize with others who had the same. What would've happened if I'd had no idea what it felt like to not want to be alive? I probably wouldn't have even known how to be supportive, which could've driven them both to follow through on suicide. I thank God that I could feel what they were feeling just so I could give them the support they needed.

The pizza was still sitting on the table. Friend A could barely stand up and keep her eyes open, while friend B was outside on the terrace sitting on the fence, swinging her legs ten stories high, saying she'd come inside only if our other friend drank some water. I figured I'd encourage the one who was on the couch to hurry up and drink the water so that our other friend could come back inside. Once the one on the couch realized that our other friend was outside reacting to her actions, she rolled her eyes, picked the cup up, and began to drink the water.

I told the friend outside on the terrace that friend A was finally hydrating, so she came back inside, and finally, we were all back together again. As we sat at the table eating the pizza, we began to laugh at how foolish that scene must've looked.

When people around me are happy, that makes me happy too. Happiness didn't walk voluntarily down the streets where I come from. Happiness was something I've always had to create. I seemed to always make people laugh, even in the midst of misery. I would definitely rather laugh than cry—or even worse, die!

I always saw being a friend as the perfect opportunity to give life support. Eating with friends and family is one of the best feelings in the world to me. Supporting others throughout life was always something that I wanted to bring to the table.

Distractions, where I come from, were so common that they were actually what everyone was focused on. They were the way of life. The same amount of money our parents made every two weeks could be made in days and, in some cases, a few hours depending on how you played your cards.

Life growing up was a hustle. Even if you weren't making the desired amount of money for your financial goals, you were still making money on your time. It was the entrepreneurial dream—just not the right way or with the right product.

To be honest, I didn't understand that it was okay to strive for greatness or aim to get the best out of life until I had a record deal.

That's when I saw people living a good life legitimately—focused on their gifts, goals, grinds, and God. They weren't working because they had to be there, like most people working nine to five. They were working because they *wanted* to be there. They were passionate about what they were doing, and they had faith in doing it. They believed that their God-given talent was to be used with purpose. I was instilled with fear and raised to believe that I was singing for the devil, but they were taught that they were created to do this.

There are so many aspiring artists out there looking to be discovered. Everyone's all over social media paying money for likes, comments, and followers. They're on survival mode looking for handouts, shortcuts, and recognition—or wishing on a star with a dollar and a dream. It's not easy, yet I was fortunate enough to achieve one of my dreams and sign a recording contract with a major record label one year after graduating high school. It wasn't a deal that brought me fortune or fame; it was a different kind of deal. It was the kind of deal that taught me ways outside of what my family, my friends, my hood, my school, my job, and my church ever taught me. They had me following the kind of rules that kept me living in fear.

My record deal taught me the true meaning of faith. Conditioned to go to school Monday through Friday, get a job, work nine to five, pay bills, and then fill the rest of my time with church, I was scared into disassociating myself with anyone in the world if they didn't have the same mindset. Don't get me wrong—it's a jungle out there, but having a record deal taught me the value of my art and that fear can't exist when you're standing on the line with faith. It takes a lot of faith to share your gifts with the world.

Tuning into my innermost feelings without the judgment, interruptions, or distractions from others while melodically articulating allows me to express myself authentically, giving me the understanding that *I am art*. I learned that not only is it okay to create but creating is nonnegotiable. It's mandatory! We were created by the Creator to create. It's okay to be great, it's okay to have faith, and it's okay to contribute to changing the world and making it a better place. The best things in life are created.

One of the greatest things I've learned is how to take the wheel and steer my own vehicle. Where I come from, we would all jump in the same car and ride together out of fear. We all shared a similar struggle, so it felt good to know that we had each other's back. The only problem with that is, it can sabotage our individuality. We weren't taught how to support each other when it was time to make different turns and journey on our own roads.

Having a record deal, although it wasn't a big deal, was kind of a big deal for me. It was a combination of having a job, a career, attending a school of the arts, and a hobby, all at the same time. I came from the School of Hard Knocks, where we weren't given direction. Most of the time, we didn't even know where we were going. We were just riding—jumping into fast cars with loud music, speeding, headed nowhere fast, wasting gas.

When you have a focus, you're less likely to go with the flow, because you have a plan. You go with the goals. Before I decided to pursue music, I was living my life trying to find my life. It gets very depressing when you're visually blind and can't see where your life is going. The clearer your vision gets, the more creative you become. As you begin to see the picture you're creating for your lifestyle vividly, everything outside of that picture is periphery.

Enjoy the journey while you're in drive mode: the lights, the cameras, the action. As much as possible, live your life with passion. Dream big, love hard, turn the music up, travel, work smart, and give it up to the Creator—that's where you'll find your peace. A supreme level of focus is necessary to reach your destination. If you take your eyes off the road for too long while in motion, you will lose control, lose momentum, lose focus, lose sight of where you're going, lose your drive, and possibly crash.

The vision of creating music that would inspire people all over the world to live their best lives is what keeps me driven, but unfortunately, there are other things that come up that may require my attention. There are good distractions as well as bad distractions. I've paved way too often for the bad distractions, and these things have led me into this dark place. When I can see the light at the end of the road after being in a dark place for so long, it's my time. That's what I like to call *tunnel vision*. That's my green light indicating that it's go time! That green light at the end of the tunnel is the traffic light of your life.

One time I saw the light and it scared me. It was a sign for me to stay focused, but the thought of something so good made me start feeling like I was driving toward my death, so I panicked and turned the other way. I literally changed directions and started running back to where I came from. I was still driven, but now I was driven by fear. Months later, I'd gotten nowhere. I slipped into depression. As time went by, I realized how much I'd allowed fear to destroy my destiny.

Sometimes we manipulate our momentum because, although we want to reach our destination, we're scared of leaving what's behind us. We try to stand on two grounds in fear of letting go of the past, but destiny requires us to let go of the past before it hands us the future.

FEAR is an acronym that has two sides: *Forget Everything And Run and Face Everything And Ride.* Moving backward isn't what was intended for us when we were created. Sometimes we have to take a few steps backs in order to move forward, but running away keeps you from reaching your destination. We were made with our heads straight, looking ahead, not backward. We are supposed to look ahead and move forward even through our fears. Go confidently in the direction of your destiny. Face everything and rise!

Have you ever thought about why you were created? What keeps you driven? Do you know where you're going? Have you pictured in your mind a destination that excites you? When you think about purchasing your favorite vehicle, you think about the make and the model, the year, the style, the color, the size, and the price to pay. Do you think about where you're going, who's riding with you, and if you would be okay riding alone if your company doesn't want to go to the same place you're going or take the same route? Is the person in your passenger seat *driven*? Can your passengers take the wheel and continue to steer you in the right direction, or will they steer you down the wrong path? Do you roll with backseat drivers—you know, the people who always have something to say but are laid up in the backseat with no drive or no vehicle?

We have to be mindful of those we are surrounded by. Some people will pull us away from our dreams into their own dreams, while others are destined to give us the map and put us on the road toward our own journey. When you have a destiny, you will see things that others may not see. It can be scary, but that's your confirmation that it's only for you to see. Once you know where you're going, it's time to take off.

Destiny will sometimes shift your circle of influence from the ones who pull you away from your purpose to the ones who push you closer. You can tell who allows their fears to encourage them to face everything and ride just by who you become when you're around them. When you're rolling with the riders, you won't run into a dead end and then park. There will be rocky roads, but the travel will have an itinerary that gives you the vision to stay driven. You will feel the difference. You'll become more productive and less distracted, more loving and less hateful. You'll be happier and less angry. You'll have less of an urge to control others and pull them into your needs and more of an urge to support them with theirs.

When you come across others who allow their fears to cause them to forget everything and run, the journey won't be the same. They see a problem for every solution because their fear affects them by scaring them off the road. This type of fear has you focused on all of the reasons why you should stop. The runners have a different focus than the riders. The riders create solutions for problems so that they can stay driven, because no matter what, their goal is to reach the finish line. Riders do it even when they're scared.

When you are in alignment with your company, you'll be driven to push one another as far into your destiny as you can possibly go. Fear can cause you to grasp, hold others back, or pull them closer toward you, but love is the driving force that allows you to support whatever it is they have to do. Love always welcomes you back with open arms as long as the departure is in pursuit of destiny.

Some of us are riding around in circles because we're not intentional with our drive. Some of us drive around chasing things—like money, for example. Money is the root of all problems for some people, while lack of money is the root of all problems for others. We need money in order to live our lifestyles, but we do not need money in order to have breath for life. Chasing money will cause you to push it away. Think about it: if you're chasing something, that means it's running away.

When you're driven by purpose, you become a magnet. You won't have to chase anything. You will attract it. It will come to you when you increase your value by developing your abilities, perfecting your craft, furthering your education, contributing to the world, and just striving to become a better person in general.

The money, the relationships, the careers, the answers to the questions you've been searching for will come to you when you allow yourself to listen. Sometimes you have to close your eyes in order to hear. Our brains are literally cameras, taking pictures of the events that happen throughout our lives. Many things stay in our head because we keep recapturing these moments.

Pictures in our head of things of the past don't actually exist in the current moment. They are not actually happening in the now. They actually no longer exist, but we tend to still picture these things when our goal should be to remove these pictures and clear our mind so that we can visualize what we could create in that empty space.

CHAPTER 3

Song of Purpose

Sitting in the basement studio of a multimillionaire producer extraordinaire, staring at the plaques on his wall, predicting my placements while setting my vibes, is how I began this particular session. This happened in 1994. I was still a senior in high school, but although I was on the runway preparing for takeoff in the flight of graduation, awards and music plaques were actually the diplomas that had my interest.

In order for me to begin the writing process, I need to *feel*. I need to visualize a picture so that I can develop a concept in my head. It's like a portrait, except the harmonies of my voice would be the paint used to color my canvas. As I sat by the soundboard composing and playing around with different melody ideas, I began see vivid ideas flow across the screen in my head.

The producer would come back downstairs every now and then to ask if I'd come up with anything yet. The answer to that question was a bit complex. It was *yes*, but *no*. Yes, I had come up with some things, but no, I hadn't come up with the thing that I needed to feel in order to begin recording. I've always had this vision that gives me the ability to see exactly what I need to see in order to take things where they need to be.

He understood. He was a creative being. He was just a bit overzealous to hear what I would come up with. But I had to stay in control of my creative space, and I didn't want to rush the process.

The producer had a beautiful house, well-mannered children, a full-blown recording studio in his basement, and a wife who took care of the home while he worked. When she came down to the studio area and invited me upstairs to join them for dinner, I knew she was nothing less than the epitome of a woman. I'd been places where people would eat in front of me and never think to offer me anything. Not that they're supposed to, but because of who I am and where I come from, I just don't feel good about myself eating in front of others if others around me aren't eating also. So I always make the offer.

His wife had no idea that if I had not been there working, I wouldn't even know where my next meal was coming from. I never let off that kind of energy. I was way happier to have the opportunity to be working in an industry that I was passionate about than to be bitter, seek pity, or have any level of resentment or jealousy because my family wasn't in that place growing up.

I've crossed paths with kids who robbed, stole, sold drugs, took drugs, overdosed, danced naked, had sex for quick money, and worst of all, killed if they had to. I understood why they did it: life is not a song and dance for everyone. Because of my circumstances, I decided to sell weed at one point, and it brought in quick money for me, but the person I had to become robbed me of the person I wanted to become. That person stole my focus from what I was truly passionate about, so I stopped selling weed and put everything into my music career. I knew that if I could sit and eat with millionaires, I could also work to become a millionaire.

It definitely wasn't likely for any of us who came from the hood to reach that seven-figure mark, but I saw with my own eyes that it was possible. This studio session was a pivotal moment in my life. I began to realize at that time how powerful music is.

This particular music producer not only played available tracks for me to write to but shared the emotional mindset behind each track. For instance, there was one record he played that made me feel anxious. I didn't quite know how to make sense of it, but what I can say is, it just didn't feel good. He admitted that he was in a bad place when he wrote it, coming out of an ugly breakup with an ex-girlfriend who was his high school sweetheart. He wanted to kill her for leaving him. He wasn't a killer, but he was expressing how he genuinely felt. He had put that energy into his music. Although this producer had some dope tracks, that specific track was very dark, and it affected my mood.

I expressed that it made me feel weird. More specifically, I felt what he was feeling—dark and ready to kill somebody! That's not a natural frequency for me to vibrate on, so I quickly asked him to go to the next song. I just wanted to create something that felt good. I was tired of being depressed, so I was looking for music that would inspire everyone to dance and celebrate. That's the type of music I wanted to share with the world.

He played other records that I was feeling, but for some reason, he would keep going back to this dark track and trying to convince me to write to it. I just wasn't feeling it. I wasn't in that space, so unfortunately, I left that night without completing a record.

I often felt like I was in this dark place growing up. Other times, I felt vibrant. The transition was so weird: depressed one minute, feeling stuck and lonely, then inspired the next minute, ready for the world. I would keep to myself as much as possible when I was in that dark place, almost like I was hibernating, crying in the dark, struggling with growth one minute then suddenly, the next minute, out and about, living out loud, spreading my wings, flying high.

It's not until I'm flying that I realize I've transitioned. I discover that I've just grown new wings and I'm ready to break out of my creative cocoon feeling brand new. These aren't the wings you get when you die but the wings you get when it's time to live your life and fly. I was thinking of new ideas, feeling new energy, reinventing a greater version of myself, and singing a new song, "Revised."

Whenever I'm in a dark place or feeling lonely, I embrace it, because that's exactly where God was when He created light. Since

God is the original Creator and He created us in His own image, the darkness I experience is my sign that it's time to create.

I could've spent my time chasing people who walked away. I could've spent my time running back to the very things that hurt me, just for comfort and familiarity. I chose to be alone in my dark place. I needed to know the truth about myself. Was I strong enough to stand on my own? I tend to get so attached to other people that I forget about my own strength and ability to create my own light in my darkness.

We're all unique, and we each have a different role. When we stay in our magic and tap into our God-given abilities, the journey becomes heavenly, but when we lose sight of ourselves and focus on other people, what they have, and what they are doing, we create our own hell by neglecting our purpose here on earth, just like Lucifer did in heaven.

Lucifer was known as the musical angel. He had the best voice in heaven—angelic and powerful. Lucifer was given the position of musical director in heaven by God. His voice alone could do the job of the choir. He sang every tone, every range, and could sing all sectional notes, from baritone all the way to soprano, with the ability to hit them all at the same time!

He played many different instruments: organ, harp, cello, trumpet, violin, and drums, just to name a few. He directed the choir, and the choir members sang, danced, stomped, and shouted while clapping with tambourines. Although Lucifer's voice alone could sound like a choir with his many different voices, directing the choir had a bigger purpose, which was to bring everyone together to fellowship.

Heaven was a place where the angels knew their roles, handled their responsibilities, and didn't worry about what others were doing or who they were doing it with. They all just worked in their own field, living their purpose, and then taking a music break to appreciate and show love to each other, celebrate life, and worship the Creator. No other angel had as much power in heaven as Lucifer did. He aced his job in heaven by creating different kinds of music for different purposes.

Music was used to celebrate the success of another, to mark the departure or arrival of one traveling, and to inspire the angels as they worked in the field honoring their own roles. Lucifer turned it up in heaven! He was choir director by day and DJ by night. Even when everyone differed on life goals, he knew that the music had its own level of similar tastes and interests that would bring people together in fellowship to honor God for His creation.

Music accompanies us on earth as well, from the time we wake up to the time we go to bed. Music is life! Music is used to teach because a melody makes it easier for the brain to memorize. It creates a calm and relaxing state of mind after a long day's work. Music in its most pleasant frequency can soothe even the most savage of beasts. Your heartbeat is music—it's your body's personal music box, assuring you that even when you are alone, you are alive. Feel the rhythm in your soul. Music is life!

Music is used in the bedroom while making love, and music is used in the church to praise God. How powerful is that? Music is literally the medium between the sensual and the spiritual life.

Lucifer had the best job in heaven. He lost his position as the musical angel because he tripped and fell on the other side of the thin line. He became a hater. Lucifer was so focused on what God could do that he thought he too could move that way. This made him lose sight of his own path, causing him to miss his steps so he tripped and fell. He became the fallen angel, professionally known as the devil, doing business as "the enemy."

We all have choices. The devil throws tempting choices in our face because he wants us to fall just like he did. He throws so many distractions in our face to keep us from getting ahead. Sometimes you can't tell what the right thing to do is because you're so caught up in and surrounded by wrong things. The wrong becomes the norm, and you don't even know what's right.

The enemy, formerly known as Lucifer, took his God-given power and began to use it against God after he was fired from heaven. He now creates music to distract us from living up to our highest potential or finding our purpose by evoking feelings of fear. Through fear, he is able to maintain a level of control over us. He is on a mission to use music to destroy us. That's his way of getting back at God. His aim is to keep God's children from winning.

Where I come from, I pretty much had to choose between my music career and my religion. I never understood why I had to choose when the gift I wanted to share with the world was God-given. I grew up in a Seventh-day Adventist household. I went from singing in the choir at church and praising God to having a record deal and singing R & B music about relationships worldwide. My church wasn't too supportive of secular music, so I lost the desire to attend church. And that's when I found God! My relationship with Him grew, and my purpose began to become clearer.

When you're speaking from the heart, sharing your art, your story is your ministry. When you're sharing your truth and experiences, that authenticity and honesty is what touches and heals souls. Motivating others to become a better version of themselves, or even to just stay alive—be it in church or worldwide—is all a form of art. Artistry and ministry are two of a kind.

Ministry is a natural gift that is given by those who are compelled or spiritually moved to do so. My art was God-given, and like Him, I am a creator. While it is in the Bible (Exodus 20) that God created the world in six days and rested on the seventh, I find that I don't have to choose because I can use my art and create six days a week and then rest on the seventh day.

I am very spiritual. I believe in God, and I believe that God has a purpose for all of us. Focusing on religion sometimes can be a distraction from focusing on purpose. In religion, you tend to get caught up following church rules and abiding by the family tradition in the religion, but in purpose you search for the truth—your truth, the truth of why you as an individual were born and what you should be doing while on this earth.

The enemy uses music where he knows God's people are most, and many times, it's church. Some music makes you feel amazing and inspires you to dance and sing praises, while other music is solemn and makes you think about all of the things going on in the world, afraid to feel your own vibrations. You get scared into going to church where they can control you and keep you distracted from who God created you to be. I'm not saying church isn't a good place. I'm saying the devil networks in church because his aim is to steal God's people.

I sang in church, but I got talked about because I actually enjoyed myself. Church folk would say I looked like I was at a party. Why? Because I had my two-stepping, head-bopping swag while others were scared to let loose and feel good. They'd prefer to have you crying in fear, scared of the world, attached and controlled. Some gospel music was created on a certain frequency that steals your joy and imprisons your soul. Remember, the devil once worked for God. He knows how to make music for God's people.

Every Friday night when I was growing up, my father would play music from a Christian station, and I dreaded it because it made me sad. Friday nights used to be torture for me. The music he played had me at home thinking about dead people. I thought things like *who's going die next, how are they going to die*. I wondered about people I knew who had already died and whether they were going to come get me. I was traumatized by Fridays. Which is why now on Friday nights, I have the desire to go to live music spots or lounges with DJs who play upbeat, high-frequency music that keeps me from getting depressed.

Throughout my journey, I was connected to like-minded people who were also on a mission. Love was our religion. We didn't follow church rules or claim to be holier than thou. We were just being and sharing authentic relations and good vibes with passion and love for music and each other. I happen to connect well with people who love music, make music, play music, create music, and celebrate to music.

It was always in me to express ideas and emotions through song. It's therapeutic to do so. I wasn't only concerned with singing a song, I was also concerned with the purpose that the song had and letting my voice be heard with intentions.

I don't focus on making money or winning a Grammy when I create. Of course, the money is necessary to take care of my family, and the Grammy, in a sense, is like a degree, so it would be an amazing reward for the hard work. However, my true happiness is in the creative process. Creating something out of nothing is everything. It is proof that there is a God, and He's giving me something to live for.

Even if I had never gotten a record deal or had a hit record, I would still have something bigger to keep me from slipping and selling hardcore drugs, making illegal money, and overdosing on drugs or alcohol. I had something to do when family and friends weren't emotionally available and boyfriends weren't really committed. My songs have a purpose bigger than just the charts.

Music brings everyone together after so many things separate us—like hate, religion, racism, and politics, just to name a few. When I watch the Grammy Awards and see how diverse the audience is, that, to me, is church. You see people from everywhere and every culture singing their songs and having their hearts touched by Grammy thank-you speeches. They're telling their stories in those speeches, and most of the time, I shed tears because I know the struggle. I'm inspired to see that what they've created and shared with the world has manifested. When artists get on that stage, it's like a performance of freedom.

That's heaven to me. No worries, just sincere expressions by way of art. We are all artists, and we all are great. The key is to keep a song in your heart and live your life like you're performing it onstage, because the world is your stage. We all have a testimony to be told, whether we sing it, dance it, walk it, talk it, paint it, or minister it. Live it!

CHAPTER 4

THE BOOK OF LOVE

The night I got home from listening to herstory (in chapter 1), I sat up until I saw the sun rise. I couldn't sleep. Anxiety, chills, and flashbacks seemed to want to jump into bed with me. I know everyone has a story, but many people don't have the courage tell theirs. Her story evoked some old emotions in me because there was a relatable connection that forced me to take ownership.

I'm really not too much of a conversationalist when I'm focused on something specific, simply because it could be counterproductive. I usually like to get straight to work. But that day, herstory struck a nerve.

There I was again, on my knees, praying, "Now what, God"? I couldn't sleep. I felt like God was right next to me poking me, making me feel uncomfortable in order to shift me. I finally needed to revise my own love story, because deep down inside, I wasn't happy.

Exactly what am I doing? Am I cool being in a relationship when really, we don't *relate* in this *ship*? I had my own life to live and my own dreams that I wanted to make come true, but here I was, living his life. Herstory was my story! At that point, I knew I had to start making changes. I was coaching her when clearly I needed a fix.

It was a weird time in my life. I was becoming someone new, so I was going through withdrawal. I was addicted to being loyal to the wrong person. Honestly, I thought I was wrong to walk away from someone because of our history, but that day, I realized that walking away from someone who no longer serves you any purpose will now be a part of herstory. It is a very powerful movement.

I pulled up to a mansion on Star Island where I had arranged to meet the guy I was seeing. In the beginning, we'd had a really great relationship—one of the most open, honest, and real relationships I'd ever had. He was in the music industry, working on a project, and he knew that I was in Miami with a few of my besties, so he invited me to come see him. He told me to bring them as well, as they'd be very well taken care of.

This was a really crucial time in his life. The record company he was with had released a compilation album, and it was getting a nice buzz worldwide. People from all over the world were starting to recognize his music. The hard work he'd been putting in for years was finally paying off. He was literally watching his dreams come true.

He guided my friends inside as he held my hand, bringing me inside also but toward a different part of the house. He showed my friends to a nice open place to sit and wait, offered them food and unlimited drinks, and then ushered me upstairs to his bedroom. We talked a little bit and hugged a lot.

By the look of things, it seemed as though a lot of sexual activity had been going on. What he wasn't getting from other women was the substance and emotional support that I brought to the table. I honestly didn't focus on what had happened with other women when I wasn't there. I was focused on the friendship we had whenever I was.

I was sincerely happy for him. Of course, it hurt to think of him being with other women sexually, but to build something from the ground up for years and finally see it surface was way bigger to me. People cheat and get cheated on every day, but people don't accomplish worldwide dreams every day.

I didn't mention the blond strands of hair I'd seen on his bed, the extension braid under his bed, and the naked women in another section of the mansion I'd passed while going to the bathroom. I was so focused on this guy who had a dream and shed blood, sweat, and tears to pursue it. I knew this because I was there with him, bleeding, sweating, and shedding tears as we cried together. And now, seeing his visions come to reality right before his eyes, it felt good to me to be able to support him even through my own pain.

I've always had the ability to look at the bigger picture. I have feelings and they matter; however, something much bigger was happening, and I understood and supported it.

He walked me and my friends out to the car as we were leaving. While we were walking, I heard some of the females saying, "Who's that? Is that his girlfriend?" and I could see the looks from different fans wondering who I was to him.

He leaned over to hug me, but at the same time, he looked like he didn't want to lose the groupie love. I could tell that all of the females around him were giving a nice boost to his ego, and I guess he needed that in order to continue to thrive. I gave him a casual hug and then politely pushed him away. He looked at me wondering why but also with a sense of excitement, like, "Oh, she gets it!"

I told him that I was very proud of him, but since there were so many females surrounding us, I didn't want to rain on his parade. He had fans. He had admirers. He had groupies. They didn't have to know how close we were and that we had a very understanding friendship. What I wanted them to know was that they had every right to admire him. This man was amazing! He was doing big things. We both knew what we were to each other.

I didn't want him to have any worries on his mind, so I smiled and told him that we'd talk later and not to worry about me. I said, "They don't have to know who I am. You know who I am, and that's all that matters. Those are your fans, and the only reason you have them is because aside from you looking good, they admire your work. Go entertain your fans, and I'll see you later."

He looked at me and said, "You're so dope for this. I'll see you back in New York." He watched me as I walked away.

I walked away from a hurtful situation being happy for someone I loved. At that very moment, I felt myself metamorphosing into a grown woman. I knew the kind of love I gave couldn't be reciprocated. I had to ask myself, *Am I loving the right person the wrong way, or am I loving the right way but just the wrong person?* He wasn't capable of giving me the kind of love I needed, so I decided not only to walk away that day but to walk out of the lane he'd tried to keep me in.

There were a few tug-of-wars, because he was strong enough to pull me back a few more times, but it became clear that his only reason for trying to keep me was the way I loved him. He was incapable of loving me back the same way. He had no intention of serving a purpose in my life, but he had every intention of having me serve a purpose in his.

He gave me money—a whole lot of money, actually. Don't get me wrong. He gave what he knew how to give. But what I've learned from this situation is that some people will please you just enough to keep you around for their needs.

Loving him was officially a liability. I'd be stuck in a traffic jam had I not changed directions and intentions to reach my destiny with him. He was a great person, but he was in the wrong lane of my life. It was my responsibility to clear the way and put him where he truly belonged: the friend zone. I know he was digging me, but he wasn't loving me enough to become who a man becomes when he's ready to be her king. He wasn't husband material.

Back in New York, watching his calls appear on my phone screen until the ringing stopped, I found myself in that dark place again. *Now what, God?* I always came out feeling revised after this dark place, so I was excited to see what was next. At the same time, I was blind. I couldn't see the light while in that present place.

Love has the most powerful healing energy. My pain confirmed that this wasn't the right relationship. He had no idea how bad I was hurting. He had no connection to my pain because his feelings and needs were the only thing that mattered to him.

When I tried to communicate my feelings, I was shut off, just like a light switch. The texts following his unanswered calls were all about him—what he was doing and what he needed. They were never about me and how I was feeling or my needs.

This kind of love would be considered bad business in my book. If I was investing 100 percent and he was investing 50 percent, I'd have to take away half in order to match him, get him to give another half in order to match me, settle for less, or walk away from the deal.

I chose not to resort to giving back 50 percent, because that would minimize my character. I'm not a half-stepper. Since, you can't make a cat bark, I stopped asking for more. I knew it was unnatural for him to give another 50 percent, and I wasn't going to settle. My only option was to opt out of the deal totally and find a partner who naturally matched my efforts. I need another 100 percenter. I did the work it took to be in love with myself, so I was ready to give love freely 100 percent.

Love, like a business, should be equally beneficial to both parties. Otherwise, it's not a good deal. When you have an understanding about each other's needs, there will be no misunderstandings. Anytime you have to force someone to be the kind of person you need, that takes away from the person you both actually are. That can cause a lot of resentment on both sides. The other person's lack of reciprocation will subtract from your elevation, and your ability to elevate will create a fear in that person of being left behind.

In this life of sin, there are a lot of distractions keeping us from fully loving each other. Fear is the biggest distraction from love. Nowadays, hooking up sexually is more common than building a relationship. Everybody seems to fear real relationship bonding. Fear keeps many of us from being open to learning the value of nurturing relationships and understanding the fact that family is the key to success.

Four hands are better than two. Two checks are greater than one. Two hearts aligned in love bring all of these things together as one. When you find someone who matches your style of love, you've got a good business partner. Whether you're creating babies and starting a family or birthing a business, true partnership is essential for success.

I had a studio session with a male vocalist one day. It was no different from my sessions with females. We got the work done, but before the real work kicked in, there was a much-needed therapeutic vent session.

He received a phone call in the middle of the session. It appeared that he was in a heated argument with a young lady. I would've thought it was his girlfriend, but he made it clear to me that he had many female friends, so she wasn't officially his girlfriend. He boasted and bragged about having many women, and I gave him the platform to vent with no judgment because I wanted to hear his perspective. I honestly wanted to see where all of his frustration was coming from.

He was pretty angry when he got off the phone. I wanted him to get it off his chest so that we could get back into our creative zone. Listening with an open ear gave him the green light to release way more information than we both had anticipated. He went back to his early teenage years and how he lost his virginity.

He thought he was declaring his manhood when he told me that the first time he had sex was at thirteen years old—with the babysitter, who was twenty-two. She was at his house to babysit him and his little sister who was three. One day, when his little sister went to bed, she started talking to him about sex. That led him to curiously ask more questions about sex, so she offered to show him.

I asked him if it happened again, and he said that was the last time he saw her, because she went away to college. When I asked him how he felt about that, he yelled, "Bitches ain't shit!" This is the reason he has so many. When one acts up, he goes to the next. He treats the women he deals with the same way a woman once treated him.

He's spreading sexually transmitted demons and infecting all these women. He's not standing on the side of the line that love is on; he's too scared. Love takes courage. His fear won't allow him to cross the love line, but love is the only thing that could take over the hate. In order to love, you have to remove all of the negative things that cause resentment.

This male I had the pleasure of working with was a true artist. He sang really well, he wrote and arranged, he danced, and his sense of fashion was trendsetting. He was a great conversationalist, but he was driven by fear. Many of the choices he made when dealing with women was because of lack of faith. When a man hates his situation, he takes it out on the women who love him.

It is our responsibility to make sure it is sincere love that we're bringing to the table. Drama, manipulation, lies, and control are all distractions to make insecure souls feel powerful—because deep down inside, they are not. The real power comes from doing the work that we need to do within ourselves. Love takes practice, just like any amazing thing.

Love is the highest state of consciousness. When you're aware of the pure frequency of love, you become the person God created you to be. You wouldn't be filled with the hateful resentment that minimizes you from your true purpose. When you're unaware of the pure frequency of love, you become who "they" have caused you to become, which isn't your true essence of being.

This artist placed a title on these women. He told them all they were his girlfriends because of his own selfish needs. He didn't love any of them; he needed them all to love him because he didn't quite grasp the concept of loving himself.

Placing a title on others can force them to subconsciously live up to certain expectations. When given a title, you can feel privileged and may want to live up to the title's duties without failing, and sometimes people place titles on you specifically to make you focus on their needs, which can cause you to lose focus on your own needs. This is how many people lose themselves—by trying to live up to other people's expectations.

Don't get me wrong. A title in its true purpose is a great way of recognizing someone's place in your life. It lets you both know where you stand with each other. Are you standing in love with purpose, on purpose? Or are you falling in love with no purpose, which would be considered by accident?

I've learned a lot from my vocal sessions turned vent sessions. I can never judge, because I totally understand that there's a reason why people are the way they are. I do try to show others a mirror, because maybe if they could see their situation from the outside looking in, they'd understand why they're the way they are and possibly take on the accountability to make changes. Nobody's perfect, but everybody has room to evolve.

Many of my clients were young females who I scouted at strip clubs. Many of the young ladies were open to growth. They were actually looking for open doors to walk through, and I wanted to be the door that would open for them so they'd be able to step into a revised lifestyle. It felt good for me to be able to render some kind of help.

I've learned that many of them are looking for love more than they're even looking for money. I also noticed that love isn't something that many of us are taught. This particular male artist I was working with was referred to me by a female stripper I gave my card to in the strip club. She told me she was dealing with someone who was trying to pursue his music and got the business card for him. She was hoping that he'd make it big and would be able to provide for her and possibly start a family.

She was a stripper, and he had abandonment issues and couldn't trust women. He wasn't taking her seriously, and there she was pushing him to become a better man. He had no intention of being with her at all. She was in love with the potential she saw in him through her own eyes. In her vision, he was her future husband. In his vision, he thought she knew he considered her a stripper and nothing else. He didn't know that to her, he was a better man. He didn't know how highly she thought of him. All she had was coitus and a dream, but unfortunately, that dream was hers alone.

Being in a relationship with someone's potential is a setup for shipwreck. We're trying to get others to be what we perceive them to be, even if that's not who they really are. Sometimes we can't see who people are because we don't care who they are. We're only concerned about what we need from them and who we want them to be. That situation was two people with issues just trying to get their needs taken care of. Neither of them was in love with the other.

Look at love like a business for a moment. If you knew the more work you put in, the more money you'd get, you'd find the time to put the work in, right? If you knew for a fact that someone would love you back the exact same way you loved them, you'd let yourself love them, right? Love is an investment. If you're giving love and it's not being reciprocated, that person is a love liability. If you're receiving just as much or more love from someone than you're giving, that person is a love asset. Keep them around—not to misuse them but to use them in their correct purpose and love them back. That's when your love is worth giving.

That's what we're here for—to use the people we love. Think about it. If we use people we don't love, we're misusing them, because we don't even love them.

Who wrote the book of love? What is love? We all have our own meaning and define love from the level we're on. It's easy to identify love when someone speaks your love language or loves you the way you love them. When the affection is so authentic that the desire to fulfill each other's needs is effortless, and when giving and doing is a pleasure and not a task, that's love to me.

We are all individuals and have our own ways of showing love. Communicating respectfully is the only thing that will allow us to learn more about our differences as individuals. Not arguing but conversing with an open mind and intentions will help you learn and understand your lover.

Love does not *create* problems for solutions. Love *is* the solution for the problems. If you ever feel confused in your relationship and can't pinpoint the problem, that's a sign. It could be many things, but one important thing to consider is that your lover is not standing on the same side of the line as you are.

When others recognize that you love them but don't feel the exact same way, it's easier for them to pull you out of the love and into their frequency. Why would they do this? Because they're attached. You're bringing something to the table that they want to hold on to, but they don't love you. They love what they need from you, so they have to pull you onto their side of the line, because that's where they stand.

When you're standing on love's side, you're vibrating on a higher frequency that they can't seem to reach. Their goal is to catch you and pull you down right where they are. Recognize the difference, because these are the things that cause drama, confusion, and heartbreak in your relationships.

Many times, people are aware of what they're doing. When some can't rise to the occasion, it doesn't feel good. They become resentful, quick to anger, and destructive. They have issues preventing them from loving you the way you love them. They may even have issues loving themselves on a higher level.

In order to love and be loved, you have to eliminate the things that scare love away—insecurities, blame, displaced anger, judgment, abandonment, jealousy, trust, low self-esteem, toxicity, dysfunction, and even unequally yoked sex. Love recognizes love. As you begin to destroy the distractions, you'll be able to better identify when someone has an agenda or if you both are on the same page in the Book of Love.

In marriage, the love must be strong enough to allow yourselves to become who you need to be in order to keep the love thriving. When it gets tough, only love will allow you to grow through it together—even if that means you have to jump into the boxing ring and whip each other into shape. If you're in the ring with someone who does not play fair and is throwing sucker punches, trying to get you to hit the floor and destroy you, that isn't a good partner.

The whole point of joining together in unity is to become greater people. We won't always get along. There will be times when we will need to fight it out, and that's okay. Nothing good comes easy. Iron sharpens iron. When we fight fair, we are aiming to make each other greater beings.

When love exits a relationship—or perhaps was never there to begin with—you will become a lesser version of yourself. Always remember: love stands on its own and doesn't need anything in order to pull you in. Many people use sex to pull others in to get what they want, while others think they're being loved because they're being sexed.

Love is not sex, and sex is not love. Sex is sex, and love is love. It seems pretty simple, but it's often left unclear. If someone wants to have sex with you, it does not mean that person loves you. Love has its own place and can exist without sex. Sex has a different place and can exist without love. Sex and love were designed to live in the same place, and when they do, life actually begins.

CHAPTER 5

SEX ART

I can't speak for men, because I'm not a man. But I think I can speak for all women when I say, "The vagina should be treated in such a manner where it is pleasantly penetrated."

Men don't have vaginas, so they have no idea what women feel during sex or the emotions before and after. Men have their own needs and feel what they're feeling. Many men assume that women are feeling what they're feeling too, but the truth is, they can't even begin to imagine what really goes on inside of a woman besides their penis. Men can be taught—by the reaction of a woman, by communication with a woman, by other men who share their experience, by reading about and exploring the female anatomy and physiology—but they'll never feel what we feel.

For women, just like the moon has phases, so does sex. While a man can't have sex if he isn't erect, a woman is capable of having sex even if she isn't aroused. It doesn't necessarily mean that she's feeling pleasure, but she can physically be there to receive and allow a man his pleasure.

Sex for women occurs way before penetration even begins. For women, foreplay is not the icing on the cake. Foreplay is the cake, and sex is the icing, with a cherry on top. Foreplay is stimulation of the mind and relaxation of the soul. These components are very necessary for the female to shift into full moon phase.

The magic is in understanding your partner's setup, since everyone is wired differently. When both people involved care enough to take the time to create custom-made sex, making sure their partner's needs are being met, that is a work of art.

What is your purpose for having sex? What is your partner's purpose for having sex with you? What is it about the person you choose to have sex with? Can you trust the person you're having sex with? Does the person know what your needs are? Does the person care about your needs?

Some people actually wonder, "Why should these things even matter?" These conversations and concerns are mostly neglected because people just want to hump. Not many people are taught about sex, but this is a conversation that is needed—now more than ever before!

See, certain positions that may be desirable for a man can sabotage a woman's orgasm (and I'm pretty sure vice versa, but I can only state the facts from a vaginal perspective). Sexual gratification is all about the sincere desire to please each other and being open to learning about the person you are having sex with. What drives them crazy? How will their body move with the touch of your hands? What melody will they vocalize after you've fingered their body as if it were an instrument—because it is, and depending on how you work it, you'll get different results.

These elements are so important when engaging in sexual activity with a partner. If you're not interested in learning these things and you're having sex just for your own selfish reasons—power, control, to satisfy your own guilty pleasure—and you have no intention of being consistent or adding value to your partner's life, you really shouldn't include anyone in your sexual world.

It takes two to share such a special intimate moment. If doing these things frustrates you or you don't care about making that person a greater being, then you're not equipped for a partner. Go masturbate! Self-mastery would be more ideal for you, because what you spread to the other person is one of the worst STDs you can transfer: your demon!

Sex wasn't created to destroy anyone or leave either person distraught. If you're not spreading love, guess what you're spreading? That person will take your hateful bitterness and spread it on to the next person, and this is how we pollute the world.

Masturbation is a great way unleash your dragons, get the monkeys off your back, and eliminate toxic waste without dumping it onto anyone else. Before sexual intercourse with another being, first master yourself! That will help to boost your confidence by giving yourself the attention you deserve. Many people may disagree, but I truly see it as safe sex.

Masturbating reduces depression. It builds your immune system. It boosts cardiovascular health and gives you the opportunity to get to know yourself. It allows you to be in control of yourself, which is healthier than being in control of someone else. When you're in a good place individually, then collectively, sex will be more fulfilling.

Sexual collaboration, just like collaboration in music, is an art. When two people come together and create a quality production with equal effort, mastering the skill in conducting human activity together, sex becomes a marriage, because there are two great things that are being combined together into one greater thing.

Men may not fully understand this, but please stay with me for a moment and keep reading. Women hold the power when it comes to sex. Unfortunately, many women aren't even aware of how in control they are. Our bodies will tell us; we just have to tune in and own it, confidently. A woman has the upper hand to say what will work with her vagina and what will not work with her vagina.

By nature, men have a polygamist setup. I'm not talking about their mindset, because depending on how they were raised or what they've acquired, they can train their minds, wants, and needs according to who their hearts beat for. I'm talking about their setup. The fact that they can get many women pregnant at the same time proves that they're set up as the seed planters. Their bodies give them the ability to plant anywhere and impregnate at any time freely. It is up to women to decide whether or not we will allow them to plant in our gardens.

Women by nature are monogamists. Again, I'm not saying every woman moves with this mindset; I'm simply saying, once a woman is pregnant, she can't get pregnant again until after that pregnancy term is over. Our bodies are not equipped to plant seeds. Our setup is designed to nurture the seeds that are planted. We can only carry one man's baby at a time. We feel something entirely different than what a man feels, and so we are responsible for teaching our men what we are feeling and what works for our bodies.

Our bodies go through a cycle every month specifically to prepare for a possible pregnancy, releasing eggs that don't get fertilized when a man plants. This menstrual cycle is called the *period* for a reason. This is a period where the female goes through many different emotions, because her body is going through a lot of changes. Women lose a lot of blood, we feel weak, we're hungrier than the norm, and we're needy of support and comfort because we also feel physical changes. Some of us get cramps, swelling, nausea, and mood swings, just to name a few. To be honest, we don't feel like ourselves, because for that period, we are not ourselves.

Our bodies speak to us. Our emotions are the body's way of communicating its needs. We are not designed to move the way men move and have many different men in and out of our vaginas. What we as women choose to do for various personal reasons is another story, but it isn't natural for our psyche. This is a big part of the reason a lot of women are bitter. The way many women move sexually totally contradicts how they're feeling emotionally.

If a man could run around the world planting seeds freely in all empty gardens, why wouldn't he? If he has a lot to plant and he loves his job being a planter, what valid reason would he have not to? Women are the only ones who can change that by saying, "You are not allowed to plant in my garden."

There are planters, and there are gardeners. If you come across a planter—a man whose only intention is to plant the seed (meaning, just have sex)—you as a woman have the power to say, "You can't plant here, because I need more than that." It is our responsibility to secure the garden.

A gardener is a man who will stick around and nourish the garden after he plants the seed. After having sex, he'll stick around to make sure he is there to water the garden and help with the growth. A gardener is an artist. A gardener has no intention of leaving you destroyed. He gets it, and he makes sure you're good—not only sexually but also emotionally—after all that he's put into your body. He wants to know how your body received it. What will the growth be? Even if a baby wasn't planted, he wants to know if he's rebirthing a greater woman in you.

A planter doesn't care about your emotions, and as much as women want to be strong, equal to men, and move just like a man moves, we are women, and we do have feelings. It's very hurtful and damaging to a woman for someone to have sex with her, walk away, and never look back—or only look back when he wants more sex, with no consideration of the emotions she's left to deal with.

Gardeners want to have sex many different times, in many different ways, for many different reasons, in many different places—with the same person. A planter will have sex with many different people one time.

Sometimes, for women, sex doesn't feel good. This is why it's important to understand that a woman has phases. When a woman loves a man, even though she may not be at her full moon phase, she's still willing to support him when he is erect. She's willing to give him what he needs and be there for him, even if it isn't pleasurable vaginally for her. Although it brings her pleasure to be his peace, it can be quite uncomfortable down there, which is why creativity is very important. If a woman is willing to lay there for a man she loves, I'm pretty sure she would appreciate it if a man considered a few things.

Set a mood. Play music! Music plays a major part in the bedroom. It allows her to relax, and it distracts her from focusing on trying to force an orgasm that may not even happen because she isn't even in that phase. Music can take her places you may not be able to take her because at this particular moment, you're ready to fulfill your own sexual desire. It may be hard to think about her needs while your own needs are so big. Since she trusts you, she is willing to allow you to fulfill your sexual pleasure as long as it doesn't feel like torture for her.

Energy flows off of energy, so if you play her favorite song and she begins to dance in the sheets, that energy will flow back to you and allow you to be relaxed in order to perform with no stress on your mind.

Sometimes men get into their own heads, thinking destructive thoughts like, *Am I better than her last partner? Am I big enough?* Things like that are far from her mind. If she's with you, she's into you, and she wants to make sure you're enjoying yourself. She won't enjoy herself unless she can feel that you are, so in an unselfish way, "do you." Get into your feelings and element. If she senses that you aren't fully comfortable and in control of yourself, she may panic and wonder, *Does it feel good to him? Does he like how I feel? What is he thinking? Why is it taking him so long to release?*

If you really care about her, create a relaxing environment. Her mind shouldn't be wondering anything. Music can be an aphrodisiac and remove the general stresses we have in our heads. Being in our own heads plays no part in good sex.

Depending on what's on your mind, many different components of sex will be formed for different reasons. It's good to be aware of them ahead of time so that you'll be able to identify what's happening and create solutions.

Insecure Sex

This phase occurs when you are unsure about something. It could be that you're unsure of your role, where you stand, not knowing what's on the other person's mind, not sure of their intentions, or even a personal insecurity like your weight, stretch marks, the size of your penis, etc. When fear kicks in, all kinds of thoughts start going on in your head. If it's the first time, thoughts like, *Is this going to be a one-night stand?* may occur, and so you become scared that it could be a hit-and-run.

If there's no true communication, relations, or understanding, it's challenging to please each other or feel anything. You're too busy wondering and entertaining the thoughts in your own head. If you have to wonder, there's a high possibility that you aren't ready for each other. Sex is supposed to be phenomenal. Your mind should be right. Making love to her mind curbs the insecurities, because you're actually filling in the blanks that keep her from wondering.

Making the other person confident of your intentions and how you feel will have him or her perform 100 percent better. That's just life! We all perform better when we're confident.

Confident Sex

When you know where you stand with each other, you feel free. Communication has been on point, and there's no room left in your head to wonder. You already know everything you need to know in order to go.

If you haven't verbally communicated—because it's someone you just met or because you've known and trusted this person for years—but your connection is authentic, making you feel comfortable enough to jump straight into sex, it can be amazing! If two people have the same exact purpose for sex, if they can feel each other's sexual energy, if neither has expectations of anything else, or if both have the same expectations, the possibility of sex will be great.

Knowing that you're in good hands will allow a high level of freedom, with no holds barred. Negative thoughts are a distraction, so if neither of you has those thoughts in your head, that mental freedom is what causes confidence. You'll get more sexually out of someone you have more communication with.

Slave Sex

This literally feels like a job you can't wait to clock out of. It could be a relationship that's run its course or a situation where a woman feels obligated to lie on her back, spread her legs, and let someone have his way with her for whatever reason. I've heard about this from women who were in marriages or relationships that no longer served them any purpose.

Many times, women will have unpleasurable sex and fake orgasms in order to keep the peace, have the mortgage paid, and keep a man around for insecure reasons like they're not sure if they'll find another man who provides (financially or protectively). I've conversed with women who admit they take painkillers before sex because they need to make sure they don't upset or turn off the one they're having sex with. This type of sex is torture. It is not done with love or art. It's about agenda, selfish pleasure, or control.

Porn Star Sex

This is a total performance, where you're putting on a superficial act. If he's giving money, gifts, or anything that keeps you excited, it makes you want to ride him like a stallion.

In a relationship, where love is the thing that makes him deserve your inner porn star, role-playing is a significant part of sex sometimes because it spice things up. Nice positions, nice lingerie, and alter egos can be super sexy and fun, with possibly heavy pounding and no emotional responsibilities.

Some women feel pain, while others don't, but nevertheless, it's supposed to be fun. You get to become whoever you want to become, in the character of someone who just wants to be the best sex porn star ever. This sex scene is about acting, but the purpose is allowing each other to live a fantasy.

Emotional Sex

Sex is given in a more intense form and gets taken to another level when you're not afraid to share your innermost feelings. The more you share what you're feeling with each other, the deeper the connection. When emotions are being drawn in and transferred back and forth, the fear decreases, and the ability to comfortably share your tears and vulnerability increase.

Spiritually, your souls are connecting. You are each other's sanctuary. When you're in alignment, the emotions are so major they can overpower the sex. Having someone you can trust to share your emotions with while releasing sexually doubles the pleasure. It feels like heaven when two become one sexually and emotionally.

Freaky Sex

This is the kind of sex that can occur on command. No emotions, no morals, no purpose other than just limitless sexual pleasure. No cares, no connection, and no communication is required. Orgasmic pleasure, power, and control are the outcomes. When choking, whips and chains, golden showers, or some kind of sexual gratification are of more significance than purpose, connection, and life goals, that would be considered freaky sex.

A lot of men have used the cliché, "I want a lady in the streets and a freak in the sheets." This means, "Have morals to people in public, but please don't bring those morals to our private sex scenes." If the relationship is already established and you trust your partner, go for it! However, if there is no real relationship, and you're not too sure of the other person's intentions or reasons for choosing you for sex, it's safe to discuss that before you assume that the other person only wants freaky sex, just like you.

Baby-Making Sex

You know that feeling you get when you lie down beside someone you're in love with or passionate about and get this spark of body heat that is so electrifying that you gravitate toward each other and fit into each other's space in a way that is so natural? Sometimes, sex isn't even the intention. The plan could be to watch a movie or seek some body heat because it's cold outside, but that feeling is there, and then things begin to happen effortlessly. One leg goes up, and he goes in. There's no other place in the world at that particular moment that you'd both rather be, so you lie there in each other's arms, grinding, moaning, and living so deep in that moment that he just can't get himself to pull out, and you can't find the strength to push him out, so *boom*, a seed gets planted, and both of you are too into the moment to even go wash up.

This is the kind of sex that'll make you a baby. Not only is he planting a seed, he's watering the entire garden. This is a connectional type of sex. It's a bond, and life can be created in this moment.

Don't do this with someone you can't picture coparenting with. This type of sex is for responsible folk. All sex is actually for responsible people, but if two people agree to have freaky sex with no strings attached, that would be easier to agree on. With this kind of sex, there will definitely be more than just strings attached.

Reproduction Sex

One of the main reasons God created sex was for us to reproduce—to multiply and produce more human beings. Having sex specifically to make babies because you're ready to start a family is one of the greatest reasons to have sex. No one would be here without this type of sex.

This is a major reason why we should respect sex and the person we're having it with. After all, even when reproduction isn't a part of the plan, there's a high chance that this will occur. If it does, you should have a responsible, trustworthy partner to deal with. Reproduction sex is ideal for you if you are married or ready to start a family. Always check with your partner to make sure you both are having sex for the specific reason of creating more people.

Procreation Sex

Procreation sex doesn't necessarily have to involve reproduction, as in making new babies. It can also be about creating a greater being within each other. This type of sex is designed specifically to create a masterpiece in your partner by adding new colors to your work of art. No one is left destroyed, because you're restoring a higher vibrational energy.

Whether you're straight, gay, or bisexual, it's all about enhancement and leaving each other better off after sex than you were before. Sex is an art! It is the quality, production, expression, or realm of what is beautiful or of more than ordinary significance.

CHAPTER 6

LOVE SONG

Out and about at a lounge in Rockville Center, Long Island, New York, the feng shui was pretty smooth and the company even smoother. I needed some recreational therapy after going through a rough couple of months. I was working on an assignment that had drained the life out of me.

The people I was working with were all about the money. They weren't friends of mine, and that was okay. The real problem was they weren't good people morally, and my soul needed some authenticity. I no longer had a husband to go home and have pillow talk with, so I had to call my girls.

I take friendships seriously. Although I don't get to see my friends every day, when time allows, I need them. Emotional support in a world constantly setting off narcissistic energy that drains us emotionally is something I need and fight for in my personal life.

We ordered food, wine, and cocktails while enjoying each other's company. From time to time, a song would play that had us dancing in our seats. but for the most part, our focus was each other. We were really big on supporting each other. Although we all had a different story for our lives, we were on the same page. We could all relate to one another, and that was so liberating.

I'd left home feeling like I was headed in the direction of depression, but the DJ stole that mood with a great escape: music! His playlist was phenomenal. I got up to dance even though that wasn't what I had come to do. It had been hard for me to shake everything that was going on in my personal world, so my plan was to chop it up with my girls.

As the song ended and I began to make my approach back to my table, a John Legend song began to play. A tall, nicely built guy with a seasoned two-step approached me, lip-syncing "Ain't this what you came for? Don't you wish you came, oh," and somehow my blood seemed to heat up. I got a rush and immediately felt a little hot in my feminine area. I couldn't tell if it was sweat or if something else was wet, but the vibe was so right, I couldn't walk away.

A few songs later, we both found ourselves in this zone. Somewhere between "Sexual Healing" by Marvin Gaye and "Dangerous" by Meek Mill, there was a great level of excitation that we didn't want to break apart from. The feeling in that moment made me forget about my day-to-day stress and live in the moment.

I swear, DJs should be called MDs, as in mood doctors. This DJ knew all the right songs to play that would put me out of my misery and bring me into this state of euphoria. For a few minutes, I forgot that anyone else was around. I literally felt like the only woman in the building. Once reality crept in and I regained sight of my girls, I saw that they were on the dance floor just as lost in the music as I was.

We were all there in this other place where the music brought us, including the friend who usually sits at the table and watches our bags and coats—you know, the friend who never dances or mingles because she's not single but shows up because she loves her girls and gossip. I walked over just to check in with them all to make sure they were good, and they were great! Before I could get back to the guy I was dancing with, he walked over and asked if my friends and I wanted to go have breakfast. We'd danced until about four a.m., so technically, it was about that time.

Three of my friends were married with kids, so they passed on the offer and headed home, but my two friends who didn't have a reason to go home accepted the offer. We went to a nearby diner and had a great conversation, since there was no music playing there.

We were able to focus on each other and get to know each other. My girlfriends were included in the conversation and were able to pick up on the vibes. They gave me the green light. They didn't feel like he had any cruel intentions. He and I became really good friends for a very long time.

The very next day, which was a Saturday, a high school buddy of mine who'd become this big-time promoter called to invite me out to one of his parties. I had grown to know him all-around as a person because we had created a few songs together. He played the piano every Sunday in church, got into learning a few other instruments, and began making full songs, so we shared creative vibes on so many different levels. I knew his family and their struggles, so even though I wasn't too fond of the area in which his party would take place, I supported his grind, so I went and brought along a few friends.

As soon as we walked in, I felt nothing but nervous energy. The crowd was much different than the one from the night before. The DJ was playing hardcore rap music. I'm not talking about real hip hop—cultural music where everyone is dancing or dressed to impress and having fun—I'm talking about straight hardcore and hoodies.

Not that there's anything wrong with wearing hoodies, but when you put an effort into dressing up, it shows that you care about how other people feel. If you just throw on anything and don't care what others think, that's exactly how we feel. We feel like you don't care. When you don't care, it sets off a nervous energy. When you mix that feeling with music that creates in a dark mood, it keeps us in a place where we're all sharing our pain.

Guys stood along the walls just gawking—no smiles, friendly gestures, or conversations. My focus began to shift from wanting to dance freely to making sure nobody was about to fight or pull out a gun. They didn't do a security check for me and my girls at the door because I knew the promoter, but I could only hope that they checked everyone else thoroughly.

Those thoughts shouldn't have been on my mind. If I get all dressed up to leave my house (which I call my sanctuary) to go enjoy a night out, I shouldn't be fearful that the party will turn into a war.

What kind of thoughts are these for a grown woman who is single and ready to mingle—who expects great things out of life?

Keeping it moving, we walked into the VIP section that the promoter had reserved for us and hung out in that space. It definitely felt safer, and we felt protected with security around us.

I asked my friends to be patient for about thirty minutes before we left so I could make sure my friend, the promoter, had everything he needed. Sometimes they want to take pictures for Instagram, make introductions, or solidify some type of business etiquette, so I stuck around with that understanding.

A few minutes later, this guy walked over to me and stood directly in front of me. Although there was a gate that separated the general area from the VIP section, he was still able to make direct contact with me, eye-to-eye. No smile, no greeting, no elevator pitch: he just blurted out, "Look, I just want to fuck. Do you want to leave with me?"

I started to look around for cameras. It felt like I was being punked! He said, "I'm serious," and stared directly at me.

To avoid bruising his ego or causing any drama, I didn't say what I really wanted to say. Instead, I said, with a smile, "No thank you. I'm here with my girls."

How uncouth and disgusting was that? I know he was just being honest, but to me it was sad that he couldn't think of a more appealing way to approach me. He is who he is and does things how he does them, but had he understood the significance of finesse and respect, he would've known not to approach me like that. He wasn't a bad-looking dude, but when it comes to a woman who's looking for more, it's not that easy.

The man who had danced with me just the night before led as I followed—as well as followed my lead when I led him. Smiles and sometimes light laughter flowed between us throughout our collaboration. It was all about synchronicity and supporting each other when one missed a beat. Yesterday's gardener had more of a chance of planting seeds in my garden than tonight's planter.

That was my sign it was time to leave. I wasn't mad, I was just moved! My girlfriends saw the look on my face and knew *time's up!*

I went home and started making music. As a songwriter, I want to create the type of music that brings out good feelings. I want to create songs that bring back that love vibe.

I began to think about the producer I'd met many years earlier who played a track for me that made me feel anxious. The music in that club put me in a similar mood. I wondered what frequency that music was on. I know I didn't feel sexy vibes. Some music gives off a poor sense of direction, encouraging people to feel strong even in their wrong.

Some music can get listeners thinking like prisoners of a certain consciousness, lowering the vibration by destructively entraining thoughts of disunity, disharmony, and disruption. I want to create the totally opposite feeling when I create music. I'm all about unity, harmony, and curbing disruption so that we can focus on what we were born to do, which is to love.

Other musical frequencies can stimulate the controlling organ to cause war. The type of music that gives someone the confidence to walk over to a woman without holding any type of conversation and ask for sex with nothing else to offer is grounds for war, from my perspective. It manipulates the brain to believe that this is perfectly okay, but truly, it feels like robbery. He is trying to feel her out to see if he can steal her jewels.

When a female doesn't know any better, she confuses that with "He likes me" and gets excited to give up the goods. She's being flattered into giving her jewels away. When a woman knows herself and her worth, she won't let others have anything they don't deserve.

We create music based on the level we're on, and if we're suffering or hurting, we will express that by way of music. I like to emote creatively, because for me, it's better to write a song about how I feel than to act out how I feel if it isn't a good feeling.

The adverse effect to that is, it could cause others to act out how they're feeling if they aren't creative like the composer of the song. If they don't have a song to write, they can possibly find somebody to hurt subconsciously. I'm a work in progress, but I am trying not to write songs that would set that mood.

That night inspired me to think and wonder, *Where is the art in music? Where's the art in love? Where's the art in sex?* The beautiful things that were created by God for multiple purposes are being misused by humans because they aim to destroy other humans. There are frequencies that can be used to attract love and enhance communication. Certain music will heal damaged relationships because it intentionally elevates the level of consciousness, bringing us back to our purest state of serenity, beauty, and love.

God created us in His own image, which is to create, yet people choose to go the route of the hater, the devil, and destroy other people's dreams, love, and music out of a desire to distract them from revising their lifestyles.

The night this episode took place, I didn't feel like I was being identified in my true essence. I felt objectified. He literally asked me if he could use me for sex with nothing to offer in return. Not that I'm a prostitute, but at least with a prostitute, you know you have to pay for it. He tried to get a freebie out of me. He didn't want to take the time to get to know me. He just wanted what he wanted without caring about what I wanted.

Out of all the women in that club, what made him ask me? Was he sexually attracted to me? Did I look desperate? Maybe he approached every woman he thought was alone and was rejected. Maybe he just crossed his fingers, believed in himself, and chased his dreams. That may have been my purpose for being there that night—to politely reject him and share this story. I can't make these things up; I wish I was. God puts me in situations in which he knows he'll have my back.

I don't knock any genre of music, because all musicians have their own purpose, but this was a pivotal moment in my life because I knew that I needed to write this book and focus more on creating love songs. The world can use a lot more of two things: real love and good music.

God created music for many different reasons. The Bible talks about upbeat, celebratory music and so many beautiful instruments like the tambourine, drums, flute, trumpets, harps, and lyre, just to name a few that were used to praise Him, to celebrate life, and to uplift others. Music was created to allow us to feel free in spirit and in love. Think about it: why don't we crave this natural music? It's because we're damaged and addicted to being damaged. It's so normal that the good stuff won't suffice. It's taboo. It's corny. It's not marketable, but it's authentic.

Back to work, at a writing session at Daddy's House (a recording studio owned by Sean "Diddy" Combs in midtown Manhattan), the producer I was working with on this particular day taught me something that changed my whole style of song. I spent about thirty minutes writing to his track. After I got the song to a place where I felt comfortable enough to start building on it, I told him that I had come up with an idea and was ready to lay it down.

I went into the vocal booth and began to sing my heart out. I had my harmonies all set, and I was even putting together some light dance moves that I thought went with the lyrics. Next thing I knew, the producer stopped the music and asked me, "What are you doing?"

I looked at him, wondering, *What does he mean, what am I doing? I'm standing in a studio recording booth singing the song I just wrote to his track. What could he possibly mean?* I decided to keep my mouth shut and observe, because I was curious as to what he was really trying to say. I just stood there, looked at him, and waited for more feedback. I guess he felt my confused energy since I didn't say anything, so he told me to come out of the booth for a minute.

He said, "Let me explain something to you. When I close my eyes, I want to picture myself with a beautiful, sexy woman I'm about to get sexually intimate with. I don't want to picture a woman wearing a choir robe singing at church. This is an R & B record, not a church song." He then played a part of the song where I used a softer tone. He closed his eyes and said, "I want to hear more of this. You have a dope voice, but stop doing all that stuff with it."

I looked at him and felt his sincerity. He had his eyes closed and pointed to the part where I used a smooth, airy tone with not much vibrato. That's when I realized that there was a formula to creating a love song. I needed to get out of my own way, stop putting so many riffs and runs into the song, and add some passion.

I was in that booth singing out loud, riffing all over the place, doing "me," not realizing that sometimes it's not about me or my vocal capabilities but about how I'm making the listener feel. I got back in the recording booth and began to sing in a less aggressive, vocally dope way and in a more passionate, loving, sensual way. The producer's reaction was that of a savage beast being soothed by the charms of the tone of my voice. His eyes were closed, and he was like, *Yes. This is it.*

At that point, I realized how different tones evoke different emotions, just like when you use your voice to speak. I began to think before I sang. It all started to make sense to me. I had to start thinking about what I was trying to get across in a song before singing it, because it can be very confusing if someone puts on a love song to get in the mood but the song feels like gospel. People may not be at a place where they want to cry or pour their heart out to God if they're in the bedroom trying to have sex.

That was a pivotal moment in my life. My level of awareness changed, and the way I created songs was different. I knew when to sing full and loud, but I also knew when to sing nice and soft.

Many artists who sing really well are underrated. Most people can't relate to the vocal techniques that real singers deliver. They feel more of a connection to songs with a nice melody and a pleasing tone. From a love song point of view, many times it's not about how well you can sing and the technique, it's about how you make people feel.

People want to feel good, and they want to feel loved. Sometimes hearing a strong voice with vibratos and riffs can confuse the feeling of someone loving you with someone yelling at you trying to make you do or feel something that you don't want to feel—like mad, angry, or bitter. Sometimes people want to feel free, happy, sexy. Sometimes they just want to escape from their misery.

Love songs have gotten most people through bad relationships. Nowadays, a lot of people don't want to nourish and build relationships. They don't want to be in love.

Music makes people want to floss and front like their lives are perfect and make it seem like they're living a grand lifestyle, but unfortunately, the suicide rate has risen. Everyone wants the sex without the love. We want what we want with nothing to give.

Why is it that love is so taboo when that's what we were created to do? It's bad enough that we're being torn down and stressed out, living in the rat race with so many bills, taxes, racism, laws, rules, and hate. How can we create more waves of love? How can we bring back that real love and good music?

I feel like the world is in a state of confusion. The reason for this is the heart wants to love, but our minds are being taught to focus on everything *but* love.

CHAPTER 7

BLACK LACE

"I'm in love!" she said. "I met someone who brought me to a place where I can take a peek at life through a different perspective, and it scares me a lot. I always dive deep, headfirst, fearlessly when it comes to relationships, but this one? This is no ordinary situation."

We were in studio Q1 at the Quad Studios, right in the heart of Times Square, getting the levels for her vocals together using the Digi design Icon 32 channel mixing board while she peeked out of the glass window in the recording booth to see if I was paying attention. She saw me looking at her. I saw her looking at me. We both know that this conversation was a must-have. She knew that I was all in, and so she went on.

"He's very secure, with a high level of sensitivity," she explained. "He's observative, and aside from being smooth and attractive, he pays attention. I love the way he loves me. He listens! He's one of those listeners who responds with intentions to understand and with sincere care to give a non-agenda type of reply. He never cuts me off or tries to make things about him. He gets me. I'm so in love.

"He's different from what I'm used to. He's an Australian white guy who owns the recording studio I work out of from time to time. Out of all the men I've dated, I love who I become the most when I'm with him. He doesn't give me one ounce of nervous energy when

I talk about the things I'm truly passionate about. He always makes me feel like no matter how big I dream, it's obtainable.

"Many of my past relationships ended because I didn't like the woman I'd become. When a man tries to break me down and keep me on the ground just for his comfort, constantly complains, and fights for my attention without giving me any, that actually drains me. Whereas not only does this guy support my whole existence, he actually invests in me."

I knew that this quality in a man was a major reason to hold on. That's not something you find every day, so I asked her if she felt 100 percent supported culturally.

"Honestly, I do!" she replied. "I never felt judged or like he has secret reservations about us. He openly asks about things he's never experienced. He even tried to sew my weave in for me. He's open-minded. Not only is he white, he's millionaire. He has a lot going on. I caught myself trying to sabotage our relationship a few times out of fear, and he calls my bluff every time.

"I try to push him away, but he holds on tighter. I'm not used to what he brings to the table. He's not only all about what he wants from me. He's also about how he can add value to my life. For instance, I'm walking on a journey. Some people stand in my way or even try to pull me into their stuff, but he walks beside me, holding my hand for me to step over hurdles as if he wants company because he's going that way too.

"It's so weird," she told me. "I feel so free when I'm with him, yet I'm scared about whether or not his family will look down on me coming from where I come from, and if my family will act funny to him since they can't relate to his mindset or bank account. Once people know your net worth, their expectations automatically rise because of the neediness in their lives, and they see that person as the one they can get what they need from, not giving them a fair chance at getting to know who they are as an individual. I got a chance to know him and love him for who he is, but my fear is that the people around us won't understand that.

"One thing we both have in common is we don't judge each other. We speak the same love language, and we actually both listen with the intention of understanding each other. It feels so good to know that he's like me in that sense. It feels so good to be given a fair shot and not be treated how the average white person would treat the average black person.

"I'm open-minded, free-spirited, and crazy, while he is more conservative. He's so intrigued by my exotic nature, while I love that he's laid-back enough to receive it. Our worlds are so different than what society is used to seeing that I tend to want to move in silence. I'm just not sure that we can be ourselves in public. I can't stand the hate! I feel like I'm going to mess it up," she confessed.

I understood that it was scary, but I wouldn't mess up a good thing if it didn't mess itself up. With all of the divisive spirits going on in the world, why not hold on to something that could be love? Why not just ride the wave and see where it takes you? If anything goes wrong naturally, deal with it then, but don't sabotage it because of other people's views. If something amazing is happening, let it happen!

I told her, "There could be a purpose for you two. Try not to quit before you experience the true purpose. I would explore openly and seek further, but don't live your life worrying about outsiders. Stay pray-up and let the relationship you two build do whatever it's supposed to do. How did you guys meet? What's his story?"

"I met him in the building of the recording studio," she began. "I've seen him multiple times in the lounge on the ground level. He actually popped in and out of the studio once, but we were working.

"One of the nights that I had to go to the studio just to add a few changes at a mixing session, I stopped by the lounge after recording my vocals. This particular evening, he was sitting at the bar. As soon as I sat down, I looked up just in time to catch his eyes. I ordered a shrimp Ceasar salad, and he chimed in, 'What are you drinking?' I smiled and said, 'I'll have a pinot noir.'

"The conversation was so stimulating that I didn't even want a second drink. I didn't want to be inebriated for the remainder of our conversation because, just like me, he was a great conversationalist.

I wanted to be sober once he told me he owned the building and jokingly said he was about to make one of the vacant rooms a bedroom because he was recently divorced and had left his wife the house.

"Even though I was done recording for the night, there was a slight possibility I'd go back up to the studio and get some work done, so I didn't need more than one drink. I had to stay professional, even while this personal attraction was becoming so magnetic.

"He and his ex-wife had been unhappy together for a long time. He travels a lot as an independent contractor buying properties to fix them up and sell them. He spends a lot of his time working on these projects, but his wife was more lonely than supportive. She stopped sleeping with him for years before they decided to go their separate ways. He's in need of romance. He is looking for companionship, but he's not afraid of committing, as long as it's someone who knows how to support his lifestyle.

"I felt a natural connection, because I've always supported other people who are focused on their own goals. I find that when people put themselves first and have support in what's important to them, they're not resentful, and they have great energy to bring to the table when they do come around. Even if they don't come around every day, I'd rather have their quality time over the quantity. Two or three salubrious moments a week is better than seven dysfunctional days. I'm emotionally independent, so I'm not too needy when I'm being fed with quality.

"As a dreamer," she continued, "I love when people take their time to grind, because it also gives me my time to continue to dream and work on them. A friendship based off of those similarities is what we have in common. We feed each other well!

"He was sexually frustrated, but even worst, he was so hurt. He felt like he did so much for his wife and their two kids. They were secure financially, they had everything they needed for college, with careers preset and already invested in. They traveled the world and pretty much got anything they wanted. He thought he was doing an amazing job, but I guess it will never be enough for someone who needed his time. Her loyalty grew for the one who gave her the attention she needed, not the one who showed his love by handling the responsibilities. She cheated on him, and he couldn't get over it.

"We were both at a place in our lives where we'd been hurt. Skin color didn't change the fact that we had both endured lots of pain in our past love lives. I didn't see color or money. I saw alignment, and that was what the attraction was all about.

"I only had one drink that night because I got more out of building a serious dialogue with him than the 'shits and giggles' type of talk. Don't get me wrong, I can do shits and giggles. I love to laugh and crack jokes while dancing to good music. But he didn't seem like the dancing type, and he also definitely wasn't the shits and giggles type. He was all about his business and very reserved. He just happened to be in a place where he was open for company, and so was I.

"We ended the night after two hours," she recalled. "He offered me his number and asked me to call him. He admitted that if he took my number, he probably wouldn't make the effort to call. He said he was weird like that and tended to focus on the projects he was dealing with out of fear of rejection.

"He feels socially awkward, which for some reason I found attractive. It actually worked for me, because as a woman who takes pride in using my social skills where they're appreciated, I confidently took the lead. I was attracted to him following my lead. I didn't misunderstand his follow for weakness one bit. Good leaders are great followers. He was the type to hold his hand before me and gesture for me to go first, but even though I was stepping ahead of him, it was him that would lead me to do so.

"I gave it some time, before I called. I wanted to process everything. I wanted to know exactly how I felt about the him and where the conversation went before I made the move. I try to move strategically with intentional behavior.

"Finally, after three days, I called. Once he knew it was me, he smiled. I know, smiles are silent, but I felt the energy. Before I could even say another word, he said, 'Are you hungry?' Even if I wanted to wait a while before going out with him, just to secure myself emotionally, how could I say no to a question like that when I was famished?

"'Where would you like to go?' he asked, so I said, 'There's this spot on Nautical Mile out here in Long Island that …' He broke in and said, 'Or how about we jump on my private jet and fly somewhere for dinner? I will send you home with nothing short of a full stomach. You will go home full in mind, body, and soul—that is, if you decide you even want to go home after we're done dining.'

"How do you respond to that? Private jet, pinot noir, and strong arms wrapped around me along with a comforter had my heart singing. It was all a dream. I used to read *Word Up* magazine. Now I'm flying in the sky to a place I've never seen. What does this mean?"

I looked at her and wondered why we always question our situations when things feel too good to be true—as if we don't deserve extraordinary. Coming from a place of dysfunction, she wasn't used to the good life. She would find herself pushing great things away because of fear of the unknown. She found it challenging to appreciate the peace that he brought into her life because dining in chaos was the norm for her. Her struggle between her comfort zone and her evolution was real. Although it was a tremendous fight, deep down inside, she was ready.

The music industry had been going through a lot of changes. Yet music was all she knew. Royalties from songs she had written brought food to the table. Music paid her bills. Music was what kept her driven to keep living. Music had saved her life, yet she wasn't making money with her music like she used to.

How do you make the transition from one place to another when you've been caught up in the matrix? Everything outside of the music world was so foreign to her. Ever since she graduated high school, music was her interest. Now she had finally met someone who was able to understand her whole existence, someone who wasn't trying to destroy her foundation but build it back up. He didn't want her to lose herself and go get a nine-to-five to build someone else's business. He wanted her to continue to build herself up. He didn't try to domesticate her. He compliments her style.

"The looks and silly comments when others saw us together were insane. Many times, I was ready to snap at someone, but he was just so gracefully mannered. He welcomed the hate. He knew others just weren't happy with themselves, and he rarely let it get him down. He'd lost his marriage and the woman he thought he'd be spending the rest of his life with. He didn't think he'd fully recover after that, but since he did, everything that happened to him had nothing on those feelings he'd just recovered from.

"What was different about him than the others? He didn't try to change me. He wasn't controlling. The more defensive about heavy issues I was, the more he loved me. He healed me, and that is what I have been searching for, for most of my life. He fed me, brought me out of my conditioned mindset, and showed me that there was so much more to life than what I was given.

"The sex was … interesting. It was the best experience I've had; not as sexually gratifying as the last guy I was with, but definitely elevational. Everything stressful that was ever on my mind was never even thought of when I was in the bed with him. All negative thoughts—out of sight, out of mind! He removed me from a distracted place physically by flying me somewhere new. He replaced my fear of the unknown with knowledge. Anything that would distract me from having a clear mind, he got rid of.

"He, out of everyone, deserved my sex. He did so much for my life that I wasn't even thinking about my own sexual pleasure. I just needed him to get the romance he'd been missing for so long. Sex with him was nurturing. It flowed like a river, so smooth and moist. Never a dry moment."

I knew that she had been at the point in her life where she was ready to give up on love, but after meeting this guy, she saw things from a different perspective. She went from moving in fear to walking by faith. She was now ready to create a new way and give up the old. Fuck fear, fuck racism, fuck anything that makes you subconsciously develop hatred for anyone different from you.

Marriage wasn't the only thing she'd seek in her relationships. Purpose was where her interest lay. She knew she couldn't marry everyone, but she knew everyone had a purpose on this earth, and if they crossed paths, they must have a purpose in her life.

She chose to stand in love with this man because he deserved it. He changed her whole world because she was ready for what he had to offer. They were both in the right place at the right time, physically and in the mental space.

He fell in love with her creative spirit, but he also knew that the music industry wasn't the same anymore when it came down to investing money. Nevertheless, he loved the fact that she was so passionate about everything she did without the dollar on her mind.

They built a strong relationship. They had both mastered riding their own waves in the sea of life, so when it came down to sailing ships, they rode together in one of the most solid ships invented: a partnership.

They'd had sex a few times already, so now she was at a place of comfort. She felt confident enough that they were on the same page. He made it to, and stuck around past, the third hit, so she was now ready to lace him.

When a man speaks, listen! He told her about his sex life with his ex-wife. It was very ordinary and missionary for the most part. There's nothing wrong with missionary sex, in my eyes, but I felt that for him, there was a deeper problem.

He was a good man, and he sincerely didn't want to trash his ex-wife, but he felt absolutely no connection or affection. The way my friend told herstory, it was as if he was sexually active with a doll. She felt he needed life in the bedroom, and she wanted to be the one to give it to him.

"Day one sex: I didn't do too much on purpose," she explained. "That was my way of getting to know him on an intimate level. I wanted to observe how he would orchestrate the sex scene, so I let him take control. His focus seemed to be the travel, the scenery, the private jet, a different country, his money, and some degree of control because of what he could make happen. This was a breath of fresh air, because I needed an environmental change. I also needed a change of position. I was so used to being in control of everything. It felt good for someone else to take me for a ride so that I could relax in the back seat.

"Day two sex: we were both inebriated and tired from painting the town all day. By the time we got into bed, neither one of us had any energy left, so we cuddled and fell asleep. We both woke up electrified in body heat, so we had coitus. He came before I did, but then he finished me off with cunnilingus pleasures, so was I mad? Absolutely not!

"Day three sex: it was kind of weird, I can't lie. Maybe he's used to simplicity in the bedroom. I get it! Again, I let him do what was comfortable for him. I was happy to have him in my life. He's an amazing guy. He's not a coward. He didn't run away out of fear like many men do. He's not a planter. He gardens my soil. He's ready for me!

"Day four sex: as we sat at the dinner table, I kept gazing into his eyes as he looked back into mine with curious glimpses. I could feel he was wondering what I was up to, so it was time to make myself clear. The minute the waitress walked away after ordering our appetizers, I threw my black lace v-string on the table next to his plate. He took a peek at it and then quickly looked up at me. Typically, this would mean, 'Meet me in the bathroom for a nice quick and wild sex session before anyone notices.' But this guy was different. He grabbed the v-string and put it in his pocket to avoid embarrassment. I caught his vibe. He wasn't ready for that yet, so I had to move forward with plan B.

"I didn't say a word as he sat there eating his appetizer. I just ordered a glass of pinot noir wondered how he was going to look in my bed. This was all foreplay. This was my way of learning what he liked and what he didn't like. It was also my opportunity to give him something he'd never had.

"'C'mon, Let's go,' I said finally. He asked why we were leaving the restaurant when we hadn't even eaten. I said, 'I cooked for you. The black lace I threw on the table was part of the appetizer. The bill is already covered, and the main course will be at my place. I got you tonight!'"

"We got to my apartment, and he smelled the food from outside of the door. I had a big Thanksgiving turkey in the oven. I'd cooked mac 'n' cheese, candied yams, rice and peas, collard greens, and stuffing earlier that day with the intention of ending the night at my place.

"I'm not going to lie: I thought we would've had sex in the bathroom at the restaurant, but he seemed a little pressured, so I moved forward knowing that one way or another, he was going to get it. There's nothing better than soul food except soul sex immediately after.

"Black people tend to over-season the food a bit, but we clean it thoroughly and spice it up so that every bite will remind you that we put in some extra time and love, not only to taste good but so you can feel good. Same thing with the sex. I needed him to know how much I cared about him. I needed him to know that I was not after his status or bank account. I needed him to know that after he'd fed me with the nourishment that I'd been needing, I wanted to reciprocate that right back to him. I fed him well and then fucked him better!

"He wasn't like one of the typical men who left me wondering, 'Where do we stand?' He wasn't the 'I'll be right back, I'm going to get some milk' and then never come back type of guy. This guy added so much value to my life before he even knew what my vagina smelled liked. Even if he never showed up another day in his life, feeding him and fucking him would've been a fair trade-off.

"My sex was the 'I really love you' type of sex. My focus was to give him the love he'd been longing for, for years—while climaxing at the same time, of course!

"Even though his wife had her personal needs that he was unable to fulfil, he busted his ass to make sure she was well taken care of. He thought she'd automatically appreciate that to the point where she'd love on him every chance she'd get. However, her needs were still bigger. He felt so raped. Even though she didn't care to physically touch him, he felt fucked, torn, and ripped into pieces.

"Me, on the other hand—I loved on myself so much that I had so much love to give. My pleasure came from what I could give, but my drive to give was because of the gas he put in my tank. We created a friendship of reciprocity. The more he did for me, the more I did for him, and the more I did for him, the more he did for me again, and so I brought this mindset into the bedroom.

"I put some smooth soft music on and began to give him a lap dance. I knew he'd be tired after all of the soul food, so he could relax and receive me. I started off slowly, wining to the rhythm. He began to hold my waist with his hands to pull me into him, so I reached over and put my lips on his, not really kissing but sucking. He began to use his tongue to stroke my tongue. As I kissed, he kissed back. Moving down to his nipples, as I licked, he moaned. For every action, he gave a reaction.

"He kept gesturing for me to let him in, but I wasn't ready yet. I wasn't going to let him in until I reached my full moon phase, because just as I could feel his pain when he was hurting, I wanted him to feel my peak when he was peaking. The best way to a man's heart is through his stomach, because it's comforting to his soul, so I fed his souls: soul food by mouth and black lace between the sheets.

"Day four sex was specifically for procreation. He needed a sexual healing, so I laced him with my black raw nature, and the sex was phenomenal.

She concluded, "In a world where everyone is so racist and hateful, we kept our love vibrant. We didn't become like everyone else just because they were easily influenced to be unaccepting of a biracial relationship. We didn't let anyone tear us down. We were too busy building—building ourselves up, building each other up, building on projects and assignments. He allowed me to limitlessly continue to create music in the studio of the building he owned, and I continued to shower him with love. We had two different love languages, but we understood each other's language. We built each other into greater beings.

"I was never about the dollar but always about the passion, and somehow God seemed to always bless me with the finances. This guy had never felt true passion but was always about his dollar, and God blessed him with someone he felt passion with: me."

Black lace was about the new layer of skin she developed. After being bruised, she was revived. She couldn't be with anyone who treated her any less than that, once she knew her worth. Their bedroom wasn't about power, control, guilt, and orgasms. It was about procreation. Of course, there was a high level of orgasms that would occur frequently because of the natural chemistry, but because of how the relationship developed, the focus was naturally to water each other and support each other's growth.

She wore black lace on day one, day two, and day three of their sex scenes because it covered her wounds, scars, stretchmarks, and all of her insecurities. It removed those things from his eyes so that he could focus on the fantasy, the feeling, the passion, and the love. On day four, she took the black lace off because his love made her feel free of judgment. She threw it on the table because she was ready to fuck him raw.

The true layer of black lace is when a black woman can be her truest self with another being, no matter the race, peeling off every ounce of insecurity and rising to her greatest self in a world that intentionally minimizes her. Her "visual eyes" allow her to recognize the difference in the people who free her soul and the ones who chop her wings off.

"I've never been a woman of title, and I would never complain about a man changing my status when he by far changed my life!" she told me. "We both knew what we were for one another. We had an official partnership on many different levels and didn't feel the need to sign a piece of paper to prove our love for each other. He expressed his love for me far beyond a marriage certificate, and I gave myself to him. Spiritually, we joined in unity and became one."

CHAPTER 8

RIDING YOUR OWN WAVE

Imagine being on survival mode in a deep blue sea. All those around you are trying to keep their heads above water. As you tread water, others see the power within you to stay up, so they want to get close to you, to use you to keep themselves up. The goal is to find the shore and get there safely, learning how to swim, float, surf, and tread water with less work, rather than to panic, kick, scream, or fight the waves, which is very exhausting and can cause you to drown.

Many people are concerned with the fact that the world may be overpopulated. Perhaps they've seen others drown, or people in the crowd who are too close pushing each other down, or they've experienced being pulled down by others who aim to get on top and stand above the water to survive. Others view the top as lonely. They're scared to elevate in fear of leaving the crowd, because they view fewer people as being lonely. They'd rather stay in the crowd and fight than rise to the top in peace.

It's not easy to navigate in a crowd. That's the pure definition of survival mode. People get so caught up in the ocean's emotions that they'll push you down and sabotage your float intentionally as well as unintentionally.

One of the hardest decisions in life is knowing precisely what you want. Do you want to rise to the top and swim to the shore? Do you want to stay in the sea? Do you want to stay close to others for comfort and risk being anchored? Do you want to face your fears and rise, or are you comfortable where you are?

Everyone has a different goal, but in order to keep yourself from drowning or from drowning others, you have to learn how to ride your own wave—with the understanding that others have their own waves to ride as well. Spend time with yourself. Stop accusing other people of pushing you down. When you've made the decision to swim on your own, you have to take the space you need in order to keep your head above water and breath. Otherwise, if you're close enough for panicking victims to reach you, they will take you down.

Practice doing less complaining, less feeling entitled for others to save your life, and more strategizing, learning how to focus your efforts on treading water in order to breathe. Some people use their time to build up courage, strength, and faith in order to make it to the shore safely, while others use their time searching for others they can use to keep themselves up. Many of us don't even realize that we have the power to float on our own. Some people are so scared to be lonely that they've never experienced doing things on their own.

Survival mode is all about people who are looking for life jackets. The minute they sense you can hold them up, they cling to you for a way to get what they need. If they're not giving life back in any way, they're going to weigh you down. Once they feel like they're being pulled down or are drowning around you, their gut instinct is to get away from you. This is why people come and go. When you're an anchor, they can't stay, but when you're a life jacket, you are helpful and not harmful. They have no fear or reason to leave.

Once you begin to master yourself and truly understand how to ride your own wave, that wave will bring you closer to people who can ride their own wave too. Now you have company. You're ready to start sailing ships.

A ship travels the world's oceans, carrying people or goods in support of specialized missions. Relationships, in support of each person's purposely designed mission, must be equipped to carry both parties, because guess what happens when you can't carry those you invite onto your ship? You drop them on their ass, leaving them hurt, bruised, confused, destroyed, and abandoned, just to name a few.

Many times, people come around with an agenda. You'll understand how the waves work once you master your own ship. No matter what type of ship you're sailing, whether a relationship, friendship, partnership, companionship, or entrepreneurship, these ships should flow smoothly when we first take ownership; otherwise, we create hardship.

You know that feeling you get when you're in the shower alone, handling your own business in private? When the fresh water falls down on your skin, cleansing your body of yesterday's earthly soils and making you feel brand new, you know that no one's watching you. There is no judgment, opinion, or criticism. This is why people love to sing in the shower. The shower is one of the most highly rated places where people love to sing. Even those who are not singers will admit to being a shower singer.

That's because in the shower, we are in our purest state of mind— just pure freedom of voice. Whether or not we sound good doesn't even matter. The fact is, it feels good to tune out the noise of the world, cleansing oneself of everybody else's toxicities, listening to one's own voice, and feeling one's own vibrations.

There I was again, on my knees praying to God, asking for the tools necessary to master myself. I took a social media break; I logged off of Facebook, Instagram, Twitter, LinkedIn, SoundCloud, Pinterest, YouTube, email accounts, texting, and sexing. I closed most lines of communication so that I could become one with myself. I did a lot of shower singing!

At first, the struggle was real. Sometimes, spending time with yourself is scary. You have no one to blame but the mirror. As I did more work on myself, I began to stand in love with myself instead of looking for someone else to love me. I dated myself, got to know myself, explored myself, pushed myself, built myself, and mastered myself. I meditated. I masturbated. I gave myself the love, the attention, and the orgasms I deserved.

I wined and dined myself, cried by myself, laughed alone, read to myself, self-educated, and self-medicated. I got the opportunity to know myself so well that when others tried to offer me something for their own selfish reasons, I was able to see that what they were offering didn't serve me, and I denied access gracefully.

Any man who tried to connect with me for a hookup to build his ego, to see if he could conquer me, or simply for any wrong reason was denied access. Any woman who tried to get close to me, posing as a friend just because she needed me for whatever kind of selfish agenda, with absolutely nothing to give back, was denied access. Friends with agendas who wanted me to play the role in their vision that would push them up and allow them to win—and weren't able to reciprocate the push when I needed it—were denied access.

I'm all for giving a piece of myself to others in the hope of helping them become greater, but not to a point where I run out of fuel. If they can't recognize that my attention is an investment, and they have nothing to give back, which leaves me drained, access with all due respect is denied. I need to save all the fuel I have in order to tread my own water.

Why should I have sex and give power to some guy who has nothing to offer me in return? Why should I push another woman who is so busy pulling from me that she doesn't even notice when my head is underwater and that I'm drowning, while she's standing on me to keep her crown on? Why should I expect anything from anyone when I am capable of giving these things to myself? Why should I risk pulling somebody out of their element, possibly sabotaging their wave flow, when by the grace of God, my river runs well, and I could be riding my own wave?

Meditation every morning became the norm for me. At first, it was kind of weird waking up in the morning and not picking up the phone to call anyone. I'm a people person with a free spirit that comes from a family of six brothers and sisters—same mother, same father, same household. I'm not used to dealing with things on my own, by myself, for so long. I've always found some time to get away for a moment, but in mastering myself, I learned how to get away for a while.

Discipline was one of the major things I had to work on. Fighting the urge to pick up the phone was a hard battle, but I just wanted to hear God's voice and what He had to say to me. At the day's end, laying my head down alone was a hard battle to fight. I'd been married to a man I was in a relationship with for ten years prior to our marriage. Sleeping alone was not the norm for me, but instead of looking for someone else to fulfil my needs, I had to become one with myself.

Some people believe that the best way to get over someone is to get on top of someone else, but in order for me to get to the bottom of my own stuff, I had to get on top of myself. Please don't get me wrong: I had nights where I slipped up and called other people; nights where I ran down my contact list to see who I could chill with; nights when I'd have some wine, and so the fight became harder, and I'd lose the battle, sending out some wild, drunk text messages. Nevertheless, I persisted.

Once I'd won the struggle of detachment, I found it to be quite peaceful. It was less stressful by far. Finding peace had become my number-one answer to the question, "What is success?" To me, success is being okay with yourself even after unanswered text messages, auditioning with no callback, being turned down from a job position or promotion you've applied for, close friends deciding they don't want to be your friend anymore, divorce or breaking up after a relationship, home eviction, car repossession, church disfellowship, loan denial, racial slurs and attacks, and all kinds of rejection.

It's so hard to tread yourself back up after sinking so far down into what seems like a bottomless pit. Sometimes after shipwreck, we panic out of fear and can't even concentrate on treading water, which could leave us to drown. But when we let go of the fear and let love lead, we begin to ride the waves effortlessly, because love only exists in a peaceful environment.

Love can't exist with all the kicking, screaming, biting, worrying, panicking, fearing, and fighting. These things scare love away. I'm not promoting permanent isolation or loneliness; I'm simply suggesting me-time and self-mastery in order to have some amazing energy to bring to the table when you do come together to sail in your ships. There are battleships that were designed to tear you apart and throw you in the ocean. Your job is to be able to identify these ships and sail accordingly.

People get so caught up in trying to survive that they aren't aware of the fact that they have to identify. They are too busy struggling, and the struggle is so real that it brings a level of hate to those who are on the shore, relaxing in their shades under the shade, staying away from those who throw shade.

Phrases like "Don't forget where you came from" and words like *boujee* were designed to cripple or handicap those who are capable of riding their wave from the ocean all the way to the shore. *Boujee* comes from the word *bourgeois*, which refers to a group of people who adhere to a lifestyle of luxury. People on survival mode call people headed to the shore or people already on the shore *boujee* to make them feel guilty for wanting to get out of the rat race or live more luxuriously.

Loving yourself through the hate is key to planting your feet on your surfboard so that you can continue to ride to that shore safely without letting haters pull you back into the ocean. The haters actually admire the fact that you have a vision that enables you to see the possibilities of living in the lap of luxury, as well as the fact that you're driven to live it. The problem is, they don't understand how you make going after that life or living it seem so easy when they're struggling. They don't understand the sacrifice it takes to learn how to tread water, float, and swim. They're holding on to too many things that weigh them down, whether it be fear, trying to pick others up and save them, or carrying personal baggage and insecurities.

They don't understand that it's about sacrificing. They don't want to let go of the things that make them comfortable in exchange for the things that allow them to grow. Haters don't understand how uncomfortable growth is. Haters want to live a better life too, but they don't feel they should let certain people, places, and things go in order to free their hands of the old and receive the new.

Haters will use certain key words to make you feel guilty for letting things go and moving forward, but when you're riding your own wave, you can't be responsible for their feelings. Your responsibility is to stay focused on the fact that you have to use this wave to take you to the shore, and so you can't afford to be distracted by their hateful throws. When you focus on the haters instead of riding your wave, you won't get to the shore. You'll be in the ocean in survival mode, just like them. Everyone loves company, and company gets attached, so when it's time to move forward, people feel uncomfortable.

Haters will hate. That's just what happens naturally for them because they feel what they feel. They can't help how they feel. Love your haters and be motivated by them, because you're making moves that may not be easy to make. While they can't help how they feel, some of them aren't able to control what they do.

If haters cannot get a hold of themselves and become harmful, for both of your safety, gracefully move away so that they can have their own space while you take your own space. It's important that they don't transfer their energy to you and then you transfer it right back and before you know it, neither of you will be riding any waves. You'll both be drowning in the Sea of Life.

CHAPTER 9

SALUBRIOUS VIBRATIONS

Anxiety is an emotion characterized by an unpleasant state of inner turmoil, often accompanied by nervous behavior. In less serious cases, it brings feelings of uneasiness and worry. It is a normal and healthy emotion.

Out of eight billion human beings in the world—including a big family, lots of colleagues, business associates, creative buddies, and a selective choice of friends—I look to myself for validation. I'm not too quick to blame others, and I'm always willing to check myself. If I feel anxiety around a person, place, or thing on any level, it then becomes my responsibility to acknowledge why I'm feeling what I'm feeling and to establish a treatment for it.

We all go through so many different things and are fighting a battle of some sort, so I try to make a conscious effort to analyze my own emotions, because that's how I generate the self-control I need in order to keep myself salubrious. There will be certain energies in the people around us that we can be highly sensitive to, and that can influence our fruitfulness. Emotions affect energy, and energy affects productivity. Sometimes the energy comes from ourselves— our own karma, a choice that we made—and so we're reaping the consequences.

Consciously, I keep myself in an environment in which I will receive some form of recreational therapy. A corrupted or idle mind becomes the enemy's playground. If I'm not in the studio creating, I'm in the gym inspiring and coaching others. Both places are not only therapeutic but fulfilling for me.

I don't live in the gym for the physical bodybuilding aspect. After struggling with my weight for years, with up-and-down yo-yo dieting, my fitness goals have changed. I playfully diagnosed myself with nutritional bipolarism, because one day I'm eating salads, vegetables, protein, and fruits, and then the next day, all I crave is carbs. I took fat burners and went through phases of bulimia and anorexia because of the pressure to have a certain look. I was a size 0 at one point and I was a size 20 at one point, so I can relate to every size in between.

My weight began to stabilize when I began to free up in spirit by letting go of the weight and guilt of living how others wanted me to live. My fitness goals evolved from having a six-pack to earning six figures. Managing gyms, hiring staff, training and coaching, selling gym memberships, personal training sessions, planning events, and renting out rehearsal space were all part of the action plan toward owning my own fitness and artist-development firm.

Health is wealth. It feels great to make money while getting healthy. Mental health is one of my fitness focuses: developing a strong mind, body, and spirit. When I come around others, not only do I want to look good and feel good, I want to transfer good energy so that the people around me can feel good too.

While I am strongly focused on fitness and finances, I am also very passionate about my friendships, my relationships, and my partnerships. I want all of my ships to cruise as smoothly as possible. As much as I love my alone time, I also love cruising in ships. Relationships are important to me, and I take them very seriously, because they will either make you or break you.

Healthy relationships are those that are authentically aligned— those where the partners can relate naturally and navigate with their similarities along with the gift to be able to respect each other's differences or communicate efficiently when they don't understand each other's s differences. Unhealthy relationships start with people who haven't taken the time out to check and change themselves. They haven't yet decided to ride their own wave, yet they're ready to get into everybody else's ship.

Being in an unhealthy relationship can make you feel like you aren't good enough. You find yourself confused, always wondering what you're doing wrong. Your essential needs are not being met. You even have to wonder if you're in a relationship. When people are unhappy within themselves and then you get close to them, you'll be close enough for them to spill their insecurities onto you.

A healthy individual can share insecurities without spilling them on you, and that's okay. But if you're not capable of helping people out of their insecurities, it's highly possible that they'll pull you away from where you are into their unhappy place. In that case, you lose yourself, which is unhealthy. Even if you decide to settle in that place, that's not who you really are.

An ostrich would be insecure around an eagle only if it focused on the fact that it can't fly like the eagle—but what makes the ostrich secure is that it knows itself. It knows that it is flightless and its strength is in running. An ostrich takes ownership in its powerful legs instead of using its time to wish that it had wings to fly like an eagle.

Once we know our own capabilities, we become more confident in ourselves. We then will have the ability to identify others with no shade. It's not judgment; it's understanding how others are built, what they are capable of, and where they are in their lives. Once we know these things, we can set realistic expectations.

One thing about us humans is that we assume we're all built and equipped the same, but the truth is, since we all have a different purpose, we are all set up differently. We all have strengths but understand that we also have disabilities. When we have expectations of a person who may not be able to deliver what we expect—whether they're not built for that type of delivery or not equipped for whatever reason—it can cause insecurities within that person, making them feel like a failure even though they really aren't.

An ostrich wouldn't be able to run and serve its purpose if it thought it was an eagle or tried to be like one. It would possibly think something was wrong with itself and get depressed. We thrive when we know ourselves and our capabilities. Knowing your disabilities will actually make you confident in your abilities.

When people understand what they're made of and can be confidently transparent enough to tell you that they're not capable of giving you the things you need, that level of honesty will save a lot of hurt, pain, and time—if we'd just believe them. When someone shows you who they really are, believe them! People with fear tend to manipulate their needs out of others rather than directly ask for what they want or need out of fear of rejection. They won't even give you the opportunity to say no, and they don't understand the *why* behind that no. All they know is that they want what they want, and it's easier for them to just take it. If they were confident enough to accept a sincere no, they'd be confident enough to ask.

Being aware of yourself makes you aware of when you're being manipulated or being manipulative. Identifying other people's behaviors will cause less confusion and pain in exchange for more understanding, which creates salubrious vibrations. Healthy vibes are essential for riding the waves of life, whether you're on a surfboard on top of your own wave of in a ship cruising with someone else. It's very necessary to be aware of yourself, because you are responsible for the energy you bring into your relationships.

One of the biggest reasons people cheat in relationships, friends gossip and turn on each other, and families feud is because they are not receiving the type of support they actually need. People don't take the time to get to know the people in their relationships because they think they already know everything. The perception of who they are is not the reality, and so the pressure to live up to other people's expectations rises. Sadly, they lose themselves in the process of trying to meet other people's expectations.

Whether you come from the same place or have been in each other's lives over a certain period of time, people don't really grasp the concept that we all have differences that cause us to vibrate on different frequencies. Whether you come from the same parents, the same hood, or the same religion, school, or job, you need to take the time out to listen to each other and learn about who the other person truly is. Love allows us to support each other. No matter what frequency we vibe on, we all need support, and people will go where they're supported and celebrated—even if that means leaving a marriage, friendship, or family.

When you are truly happy with yourself and secure with where you stand, even if it's at the bottom, and you want to reach a new level, you're conscious enough to know that it requires work, and you're driven enough to put the work in. When you're insecure, however, you may not fully be happy with the level you are on and may also not understand that there *are* levels. It's okay not to be on a best friend's level or a colleague's level. The insecurity may come from comparing yourself to others, thinking you can do what they can do or should be where they are. The truth is, you should embrace and enjoy where you are, and if you want to rise to the occasion of graduating to another level, do the work it takes to reach a different level the same way you have to do in school.

People who are quick to anger, fight, give up, and lose control over themselves emotionally are vibrating on a lower frequency. I'm not throwing shade; I'm shedding light. It happens to the best of us. It's all about being aware and taking full control over yourself so that you don't hurt anyone—or yourself, for that matter.

People who look for the why and search for the purpose in others tend to vibrate on higher frequencies, only because they understand the reasoning behind situations, which replaces anger. Anger removes the feeling of pleasure, and pleasure is the frivolous enjoyment in life that we all search for. The more you let go of the heavy anger that weighs you down, the higher you rise in spirit. You were born for a reason. Your job here on earth is to strive to become greater and elevate spiritually, rising up to Christ, away from the crowd.

Quality is actually greater than quantity. You can have seventy-three pennies in one hand and four quarters in the other. The pennies will be all over the place, with loose change just dropping and falling off, the same way people who have no purpose for your life do. The quarters will be stable—less change but more value. As you elevate, there may be fewer people by your side, but the quality of the people will be more solid. Most of us define ourselves by the head count we have around us, but the thing that truly matters is the purpose each head serves.

We live in a world full of lost people. There's a lot of dark energy going around. Nevertheless, it's not our fault. The enemy's goal is to steal our focus from what the Creator created us to focus on in the first place. We were created to travel and enjoy the world that was created for us to live in,—singing, dancing, praising, and celebrating God and each other. But because of the enemy, the jealousy, the hater, the devil, we were manipulated, and that caused us to go low when God wants us to go high. It makes the devil happy for us to be on the ground, but our job is to come together to generate the frequency of waves that will allow the universe to vibrate higher, bringing us back up, closer to God.

Is it really lonely at the top, or is that what the enemy wants you to believe? What does that say about how you see God? Where is your faith? With so many lost souls running around corrupting others, you'd rather stay close to them for comfort rather than trust God and rise?

The term *salubrious vibrations* means becoming healthier versions of ourselves—becoming whole and embracing new levels of consciousness in our divine souls so that we can attract wholeness in our relationships. Eat healthy, drink lots of water to cleanse yourself naturally, exercise to keep your blood flowing, find something that you absolutely love to do, and move with acts of kindness and integrity. Live life with passion and make sure the energy you have to offer is fulfilling and purposeful.

Our bodies are capable of conforming because of the neuroplasticity that we are made up of. Having the ability to change is something we are designed to do. When you meet others who shine their evolutionary light on you, that is their purpose. Many of us miss that because we are so scared of people accusing us of changing, but again, that comes from a group of people who are lost and think that would be the best way not to lose you.

It is okay to change. It's actually our job to evolve into greater beings. There is always room to grow. Life was given so that we can graduate from the old ways to the new. Grades are not only for school. Life has grades even after school is over. There are levels. Sometimes we outgrow people. Some people get left back while others get skipped. Don't be afraid to embrace the new people you meet, no matter what level you're on.

Nobody wants to lose loved ones, and nobody wants to be lonely. Everybody's looking for someone. Everybody's looking for something. Everybody wants support.

Healthy relationships support elevation. Be true to yourself and transparent to the people you love. They may not agree, but if they love you, they should be able to respect your truth and support who you are or becoming.

Love never hates and always elevates. Always try to love others through their period of growth and healing. Even if you have to love from afar to protect your peace, the best thing you can do for someone is to love them while they're getting their lives together. Always, no matter what, try the best you can to send off good vibes.

CHAPTER 10

PARAGON

You are better off to have a friend than to be all alone, for you can help each other succeed. If you fall, your friend can lift you up: but woe to them that is alone when they fall; for they hath not another to help them up.

—*Ecclesiastes 4:9-10*

Once she fully accepted the gifts she had within her, she treaded her distractions under the deep blue waves and emerged from the conflict to become victorious. Her story was revised, and a paragon was created.

Sliding in her regurgitation after an unsuccessful attempt to get her to the bathroom on time brought our friendship to the next level. We've known each other since high school but recently grew more in alignment spiritually. Over the years, we've managed to keep a friendship while maintaining our individuality. We had our own journeys, and we both understood that. We were okay living our own dreams without the urge to pull from each other—and then, life brought us closer, so that we naturally felt safe enough to open up and share our deepest stories with each other.

The transparency that came about was both frustrating and liberating. Not everyone embraces honesty, because quite often, the truth hurts. However, we were both in this place where we were strong enough to receive each other's truth.

"Were you sliding in my vomit last night?" were the words that came out of her mouth after she opened her eyes first thing in the morning. "I've never had a friend stand by my side barefooted in my vomit before," she chuckled with a tiny bit of embarrassment. "Thank you so much, because I don't know what I would've done had you not been there."

I washed my feet in her bathroom sink in order to keep an eye on her. I had one foot in the sink, trying to balance myself standing on the other, sticking my head out the bathroom door to make sure she didn't go down while laughing at how I must've looked from the outside, but feeling inside a strong sense of seriousness. I had to let her know how thankful I was that she was able to be there for me when I needed it as well.

I recognized her true greatness the moment she gave me permission to rise. She gave me the official sanction that any woman would need in order to thrive. It's not easy for women to support other women. Many women tend to look at other women to compete and compare. It felt so good to know that I had a companion on my side and not a competitor.

I can honestly say that being able to tolerate the redolence of her regurgitation, holding her hair back to keep it from getting in her face, one arm wrapped around hers to keep her from falling while I struggled to keep myself up, was an effortless reaction to having a strong component on my side.

"Cheers to life!" we had said as we sipped and toasted. I'd crashed at her house the night before, where she was able to share her ingredients for the sucker-free lemonade I needed when life handed me my lemons. Normally, we'd do wine, but last night we both had way too many of life's lemons in our system, so we decided to squeeze them into a big pitcher of vodka and make some lemon drop martinis.

We'd gone straight to her Park Slope apartment, just minutes away from the Brooklyn Bridge, after a "Women in Music" event. Another artist I had been working with invited us out to see her perform for the first time in New York.

After her performance was over, she came over and gave us both nice, tight hugs. She cried and told us how appreciative she was of the support that we came with. This was an artist I'd been working with for a few months. I saw her growth, coached her through her toxic relationships, and kept her focused on her music. We'd laughed together and cried together in the midst of the hard work. At times, she didn't think she'd make it, but through it all she persisted, and I was so happy to see her project manifest.

She was nervous and hoarse, so I brought herbal tea with ginger, honey and lemon. I walked her through sound check and made sure everything was on the same levels for her performance. From making sure her clothes, makeup, and hair were in place to making sure her spirit was free of nervous energy, I supported this artist wholeheartedly. After the tight hug came a beautiful smile and a facial expression that let me know she had something coming.

"You've been like a mother to me," she said. "I have friends that I had to cut off because they don't know how to support me the way you do. Nobody really gets me. Everybody tells me to quit trying to do music, but I have to follow my heart, and there you are telling me the same thing that my heart tells me. I need you, Asiah! Can you manage me? I need a manager that I can trust, and I trust you!"

I looked at her with tears in my eyes, because herstory was my story. I could relate to not having many people around me who understood me and so they didn't know how to support me. I totally got her. I told her I needed some time to think about it. I told her that artist management was not my expertise and that I wanted to give it some time before I gave her a solid answer.

"I recently had a major argument with my best friend," she told me. "I had to let her go because she gets mad at me when I focus on doing what I love. The other day, right before I came to see you for our vocal session, she called me *boujie*. What does that mean? Just because I want a better lifestyle for myself doesn't make me a bad person. She looked at the way I was dressed and asked me why I always have to do the most. She asked me if I'm trying to outdo her.

I don't even think about her when I buy my clothes or put them on. This is so hurtful."

She continued, "That same day when I came to see you, you told me how freaking good I looked, and then you pushed me to hit the highest note I think I've ever hit before."

Then she added, "I also had to walk away from an abusive relationship. This guy tries to control me in every way possible, but I don't want to be controlled. I just want to be supported. I love who I am becoming, and nobody around me wants me to become a better woman. They all just want me around for their selfish reasons. Most people don't get it, and you get it! I swear, Asiah, you would be the perfect person. Please think about it and let me know."

My friend and I drove across the Brooklyn Bridge looking at the scenery. I know there was a lot going on in her mind. There was a lot going on in mine too. We both do this thing where we marinate on our thoughts before we put them into words.

The minute we walked into her apartment, she blurted out, as if she had given it thought and was absolutely sure of herself, "When are you going to get yourself together? I see you doing so many things for so many people, but you're neglecting yourself. It's okay to say no sometimes. You don't have to take on every project thrown your way. You still need time to heal and get yourself where you need to be!"

I looked at her and wanted to wrap my arms so tightly around her and just squeeze her with joy and kisses—not in a sexual way, but in a way that anyone would feel about someone who just unlocked the jail cell they'd been locked up in for years.

I guess I felt guilty telling the artist no because I'd been working with her and could understand how she felt, knowing she needed a specific kind of support—and she chose me. But I also felt like I'd be putting myself off if I said yes to her. Deep down inside, I knew I couldn't do it, but I didn't want to let her down because I knew she needed me.

I was always getting pulled into so many different situations, helping others make their dreams come true. It always feels good to help others, and I never looked at that as a bad thing, but when someone can stand before you with no fear, look you in the eyes, and mirror you, showing you a piece of yourself that you can't even see, that is priceless. Her giving back to me all the help that I've been giving to others—that is purpose.

Our conversation began to elevate in a purpose-driven direction. She knew I was still silently suffering from a long-term marriage that didn't work out. She knew that I was stuck. She knew that music was a part of who I am, but the other part of me was dying and needed to be revived. I'd had to let go of everything when my marriage ended. I overcompensated working on so many different projects, but she could tell that I needed help. I needed to face my loss and recover. I needed to be a human being. I needed to build, fix my credit, get my money up, lose weight—I needed a real friend, and she was right there!

Just like I had my story, she too had hers. She felt compelled to share her story with me because she was helping me with my life, and I listened.

"I've been back in New York for a few years now, and nobody knows what I've just been through," she began. "You are the only one who comes to visit me in Brooklyn. You are the only one who doesn't take it personal when I can't respond to your text messages right away. You are the only one who picks up the phone to see if I'm okay when I don't return your phone calls, before you get on top of me for ignoring you. Nobody has any idea what I just went through. Nobody knows how fuckin' depressed I am."

The tears and the truth came out as the drinks went in. She was absolutely right—I had no idea. She definitely could have fooled me. She dressed and walked like a million bucks. I listened to herstory and would have never even imagined what she'd been dealing with. This was the first time she'd share her vulnerability with me, but one great thing that she got out of that situation was that it led her to the Bible. The detailed description of what she encountered was one that only God can bring you out of.

Her story was her testimony. You would think that it would be a contradiction to read the Bible with a nice cold lemon drop martini in your hand, but the truth is, the Bible is a book written by different prophets who were given the opportunity to share their stories and testimonies designed to guide us through our lost lives. This was a dark time for us both. We needed to be guided. Both of our batteries were drained. At that point, we needed God to be our guiding light.

As she remembered more of what happened in her relationship, her stomach began to get upset, but it wasn't because of the lemon drops she was drinking. It was the lemons dropping out of her system. We were actually sipping nice and slow. We've had way more drinks than we had this evening, and never before had I seen her puke. She started coughing and then, abruptly, she began to regurgitate. It all just came out as she relived the horrific situation she had just broken away from.

I tried to get her to the bathroom on time, but her body felt the need to release without worrying about my feet or anything else nearby. Good thing I had taken my shoes off. I struggled a bit sliding and trying to keep her up from falling. She was tipsy, but she was hurt and crying and dealing with a situation she'd conveniently put in the closet. Sometimes, when life hands us lemons, we throw them in the closet on the shelf, but they get even more sour and come out when they're ready—even on your friends!

We had something greater to focus on, however. It happened just the way it was supposed to. There was purpose. She cleaned herself up while I cleaned up the mess on the kitchen floor. We were so in the moment that we resumed our positions in the kitchen to continue, as the depth of our conversation began to reveal the purpose of the relationship she'd just escaped.

There are scriptures in the Bible that confirm that our situations were already written. You don't have to belong to a specific type of church or religion to read the Bible. When you're passionate about someone, sometimes you confuse that for love. Many times, we're not in love with the person we're passionate about. We may just have a purpose with the person.

The assignment can finish as quick as you end it, or it can take as long as you make it last. We've been taught to be loyal to people, but we haven't been taught how to identify when someone is in our life just for a season. We weren't taught to look for the reason. We just hold on out of loyalty, go with the flow, and become attached. We don't realize that there's a lesson either to be learned or to be taught, so what happens is, God begins to make the signs a bit more uncomfortable when we don't recognize or acknowledge them. We both have testimonies for days that we can share where we've found the purpose in a relationship.

Just two weeks prior to this night, I got on the Belt Parkway to drive to Brooklyn to see this guy I was dating. Although there were things I needed to know about him that he seemed to be conveniently hiding or insecure about, my current situation was, my flesh had a burning desire to be manhandled. I was hot and horny, and I needed to feel the hands of a man all over my body. I went on this date ready and willing to get laid. Mind you, this was our seventh date.

I still felt the need to know if he was sent by God to be in my life for a reason or a season, or if perhaps he was created by God specifically for me, forever. There's a big difference. I didn't want to miss the purpose with this guy just because of sexual temptations, so I said a prayer to God while speeding on the Belt Parkway to go get laid! I said, "God, if it is your will, let it be done. If it is not your will, let it not be done."

And it was not done! This guy couldn't get erect. He looked embarrassed, and he even told me that he wanted to redeem himself, but I just hugged him and kissed his neck to let him know that it's all love. I wasn't taking it personally, and I didn't want his ego to make him feel like he failed. So I spoke to the King in him to let him know it was okay. I knew that was it! I was like, *Wow, God. You couldn't have spoken to me any louder.* That message was totally heard, and I never looked back.

"Cheers, bitch!" my friend and I cried as we toasted to recognizing purpose. She pulled out her iPhone to search for a Bible verse she felt compelled to share. She usually has a different way of telling a story—very indirect, with many examples. Not that she wants to beat around the bush, but she's not quite sure she can share delicate information without it being misunderstood or misused. Most times, I have to say "What exactly happened?" because I know that I'm ready. This time, she had a spiritual way of sharing.

She began to read a few lines and then said to me, as she saw my jaw drop, "I don't know how I could be so stupid and naïve. I never let anyone have so much control over me or get the best of me like this guy did. I prayed constantly and cried almost every day after dropping my daughter off at school, asking God to show me the way. The next time I opened my Bible, I prayed first and then stumbled across the word *narcissist*. I read a few articles, but then I came across this Bible verse." She read to me the passage from 2 Timothy 3:

> This know also, that in the last days perilous times shall come.
> For men shall be lovers of their own selves, covetous, boasters, proud, blasphemers, disobedient to parents, unthankful, unholy,
> Without natural affection, trucebreakers, false accusers, incontinent, fierce, despisers of those that are good,
> Traitors, heady, high minded, lovers of pleasures more than lovers of God;
> Having a form of Godliness but denying the power thereof: from such turn away.
> For of this sort are they which creep into houses, and lead captive silly women laden with sins, led away with diver's lusts,
> Ever learning, and never able to come to the knowledge of the truth.
> Now as Jannes and Jambres withstood Moses, so do these also resist the truth: men of corrupt minds, reprobate concerning the faith.
> But they shall proceed no further: for their folly shall be manifest unto all men, as theirs also was.

But thou hast fully known my doctrine, manner of life,
purpose, faith, longsuffering, charity, patience,

Persecutions, afflictions, which came unto me at
Antioch, at Iconium, at Lystra; what persecutions I
endured: but out of them all the Lord delivered me.

Yea, and all that will live godly in Christ Jesus shall
suffer persecution.

But evil men and seducers shall wax worse and worse,
deceiving, and being deceived.

But continue thou in the things which thou hast
learned and hast been assured of, knowing of
whom thou hast learned them;

And that from a child thou hast known the holy
scriptures, which are able to make thee wise unto
salvation through faith which is in Christ Jesus.

All scripture is given by inspiration of God, and is
profitable for doctrine, for reproof, for correction,
for instruction in righteousness: That the man of
God may be perfect, thoroughly furnished unto
all good works.

Our relationship experience gave us similar results. We both had to become the men we were looking for. Not masculine; still 100 percent all woman. We still believed in love, connection, and marriage. We just had to take care of ourselves the way we wished a man would. That meant work harder, pay our own bills, give ourselves orgasms, treat ourselves well, and be great until we could find the man who was designed for us. I think I can speak for both of us when I say we were able to identify that the men we'd been seeing or dating weren't our life partners.

Women would be more submissive to men if the men of today were more of the leader type. Nobody wants to be led astray, and many times, when dealing with a narcissist, you don't even realize you're being led astray. You think you're walking in a park, with a nice breeze, hair flowing, flowers blooming, and a man right there leading you into happiness. That's what it's set up to feel like, but really, you're being manipulated into a place where he's able to control your emotions because he's not secure enough in his manhood to take the lead correctly. He's super lost, actually, using your magic for his tricks.

The night in Brooklyn with my friend was spent doing some serious retreating. We discovered some of the whys behind people doing what they do. We found an understanding so much bigger than just our own, and it became clear that the calamity of waves was designed by the enemy to distract us from what God wants us to be conscious of. It was designed to take us down and cause us to drown.

This is why we need the Bible: to guide us as we ride the catastrophic waves in our lives. I seek spiritual strength from the higher power or mentors that the universe sends my way to avoid pulling from people who aren't equipped. I'd prefer to help others stay up and be a life jacket and not an anchor.

I spend a lot of time coaching my clients from all walks of life because of how rewarding it is to be able to lift them up. Many of them are aspiring artists; some are signed artists. The females I find have been more consistent because they're seeking sisterhood, motherhood, and the type of friendship that would allow them to become better women for their relationships and their purpose. They're seeking guidance. They want to know how to utilize their power. They're seeking validation and permission to tap into their magic. They're seeking instruction on how to protect themselves from the people they love who don't support their dreams, keeping them on emotional hold and causing them an abundant amount of guilt about being who they really are.

Men go through similarities, but many of them would prefer to show strength or keep it fun, creative, and sexy on the surface rather than explore the depth of their soul. Their egos don't quite allow them to accept the level of accountability that is needed in order to break the chains holding them down, so they don't stay as consistent in our coaching sessions.

Women, however, are ready to chop the chains with a sledgehammer and rise. We take a beatdown, yet we're looked at as the light. Men have their stuff that they go through, so they come to women when they're seeking nourishment. What exactly is nourishment to a man? In many cases, sex is the first thing that comes to mind.

As women, we all have vaginas and often can be objectified and not heard. We all have a voice, yet our vaginas seem to be the center of attention. Men want to use us for their own selfish sexual needs, even if it means hurting us, even if it means overlooking the fact that we are human beings with a brain, a heart, and so many other assets.

Our breasts and our vaginas are meant to bring forth life and nourishment to the ones we are ready to build with, create with, and become one with. It's for the ones we hope that one day we can call our family. The men who plan to stick around and become our personal gardeners are the men who are deserving of our womanly goodies. Our breasts and our vaginas are not for the takers who have absolutely nothing to give back. It's very hurtful when a woman has a voice and wants to be heard, yet the people who don't want to listen to her are the very same ones who want a piece of her body.

The paragon woman is a woman who stands up for herself and strives to be the very best that she possibly can be—not looking to the left or looking to the right to see where other women are or what they're doing but looking within herself to see what she can become. The origin of the English noun *paragon* is a black stone that is used to tell the quality of gold. When you press the gold against the surface of a paragon, you find out the quality of the gold.

The worth of a man shows on his woman's face. A real man searches for a woman who knows her worth and stays driven in her own lane, doing what she knows is right and not looking for attention and affection from just anyone. He has to be able to trust his life in her hands. In order for him to trust her, she has to be accountable for her own actions. She has to be responsible. She has to do the work that it takes to rise above the temptations that the enemy is so busy trying to distract her with. She has to be conscious of these distractions so that she can recognize when to avoid them.

Remember, we are all lost children of God, so our job on earth is to find the way and become better everyday. As we conversed, I jokingly stated that we should get "Proverbs 31" T-shirts made to promote virtuous women. She looked at me, smirked and then went to Proverbs 31. As she got to Chapter 10, she read out loud:

> Who can find a virtuous woman? for her price is far above rubies.
>
> The heart of her husband doth safely trust in her, so that he shall have no need of spoil.
>
> She will do him good and not evil all the days of her life.
>
> She seeketh wool, and flax, and worketh willingly with her hands.
>
> She is like the merchants' ships; she bringeth her food from afar.
>
> She riseth also while it is yet night, and giveth meat to her household, and a portion to her maidens.
>
> She considereth a field, and buyeth it: with the fruit of her hands she planteth a vineyard.
>
> She girdeth her loins with strength, and strengtheneth her arms.
>
> She perceiveth that her merchandise is good: her candle goeth not out by night.
>
> She layeth her hands to the spindle, and her hands hold the distaff.
>
> She stretcheth out her hand to the poor; yea, she reacheth forth her hands to the needy.
>
> She is not afraid of the snow for her household: for all her household are clothed with scarlet.
>
> She maketh herself coverings of tapestry; her clothing is silk and purple.
>
> Her husband is known in the gates, when he sitteth among the elders of the land.

She maketh fine linen, and selleth it; and delivereth
girdles unto the merchant.

Strength and honor are her clothing; and she shall
rejoice in time to come.

She openeth her mouth with wisdom; and in her
tongue is the law of kindness.

She looketh well to the ways of her household, and
eateth not the bread of idleness.

Her children arise up, and call her blessed; her
husband also, and he praiseth her.

Many daughters have done virtuously, but thou
excellest them all.

Favor is deceitful, and beauty is vain: but a woman
that feareth the Lord, she shall be praised.

Give her of the fruit of her hands; and let her own
works praise her in the gates.

We were inebriated. We were hurt. We were scorned. We were
happy to begin the process of healing. As a woman who has given life
and can understand the transition from being penetrated vaginally
to the seed that's planted within—the growth process, the labor, the
delivery, the birth, and creating life—I understand the power that we
hold. So when I see women hating other women, tearing each other
down, and aiming to destroy one another, what I see is a lack of self-
love and a deep-rooted disconnect that keeps them from connecting
to their true power. If a woman has the power to create life, she has
the power to create anything. When a woman does not recognize her
power or her ability to create, she sees nothing to aim for, so she sets
out to destroy.

I dream that each and every woman reading this will strive to
become virtuous. May you be filled with so much passion that it leads
you to your purpose, and may your dreams become so vivid that you
get excited about revising your lifestyle in order to meet them. May
all of your dreams come true.

THE UNIVERSAL LAWS OF
A LIFESTYLE REVISED

1. Herstory

Some say, "There are two sides to a story." Others say, "There are three sides to a story: one side, the other side, and the truth." To be 100 percent fair, we all have our own story. We all see things from our own perspective. Not only do we all want to be heard, we want to be understood and accepted for who we are.

Write your story. Even if you're only writing in the heart of your soul, let it be written, because only then are you acknowledging it and giving it permission to exist. Right, wrong, or indifferent—your story is yours, and you have the right to have one. Writing your story doesn't have to manifest into a book, a song, or a movie. Writing it down in a personal journal or diary is a form of therapy. History has already been written, so I dedicated rule #1 to the women: "Your voice, just like your vagina, is powerful yet sensitive. Every woman has herstory!"

2. Driven

Pay attention to what gives you drive. Are you driven by fear? Are you driven by faith? Traffic rules are for general safety, but the thing that gives you drive is personal and tailor-made specifically to help you find yourself and your purpose. Don't be afraid to create new rules for yourself. Set boundaries and don't allow others or yourself to cross those boundaries. Other people are solid on their rules and boundaries, and that's totally okay. Some roads are closed to you, so you have to pave your own path. Life is a journey. Stay driven even when the road is bumpy.

3. Song of Purpose

Music is powerful. It can heal and it can destroy. It can bring us together in unity, and it can separate us and be divisive. There's nothing wrong with being under the influence of music, but pay attention to whether it influences your greater side or your lesser side. We all have both sides, and both sides can be ignited at any time. There are so many frequencies of music, and there is a purpose for every song.

Music controls your mood. When you create your playlist, how do you choose the songs? By the songs that are number one on the charts? By the songs that are on heavy rotation when you turn on the radio? For inspiration to work out, to keep you awake while driving, or to put you to sleep when you get home? Do you choose a song because it was used for a challenge on Instagram and has thousands of likes? Or is this something you never even thought about? Has music anesthetized you so that you have no idea why you even feel a certain way when a certain song plays?

Be conscious of the way your mood shifts and who you become. There is music designed to heal. When you're feeling unaligned with yourself or others around you, try separating yourself and use music for therapy.

4. The Book of Love

Are you loving the right person the wrong way, or are you loving the right way but just the wrong person? What is love? The good news is, when it comes down to the Book of Love, you hold the pen. You define love according to the frequency on which you are currently vibrating. There are levels to love, and ultimately, unconditional love will allow you to find your soul mates in friendships and relationships. When love has no condition, you get the opportunity to see who people really are, and then you can make a conscious choice to stand in love. True love doesn't want you to fall in.

Let's begin with self-love! When you forgive yourself and let go of ego, abandonment, attachment, manipulation, control, and fear, you will begin to feel true love. Once you practice self-mastery and stop resisting, you will find how powerful love is in surrendering. The love alone will cause you to rise and shine. Let go of the baggage; it only weighs you down. Love elevates.

5. Sex Art

Sex was created by God as a beautiful thing. Because we are all different and have a different purpose, we all have sex goals and different needs. Don't assume that just because you want to have sex with someone for a particular reason, that person wants to have sex with you for the same reason. Have the conversation.

Sex was created for two responsible individuals to come together to unite in a marriage—not necessarily legally or religiously but socially as well. Just like music, when two (or more) creatives collaborate on a song, it becomes a marriage. It is an art done with the intention to create something amazing. Collaborating with the right partner or people is essential for good sex.

There are so many different elements to sex. If you're not on the same page, it can be a disaster. Sex is a very intimate work of art. People have a lot of personal things they must deal with. If you have sex with those who haven't dealt with themselves, you won't find love. Just like any piece of art, sex should be done freely and done with love.

6. Love Song

My favorite solfeggio frequency is "the love frequency," which would be 528 hertz. The reason for that is because everyone in this world seems to be running around like chickens with their heads cut off—or better yet, with their hearts cut out. The world seems to solve issues with war, separation, penalties, rules, drugs, violence, and everything they can think about except the one thing we all need: love. If everybody operated out of love, we wouldn't be so caught up in the emotional vortex that gives us anxiety, depression, and all kinds of dark places.

Add your favorite love song plus two others to your playlist. That would be three love songs in total. It's just a reminder that before you get out of the car to go walk into work, before you get home, or before you get on the train to start your day, do whatever it is that you're doing with love. There's a higher possibility that you'll get the results you're looking for at work and at play.

7. Black Lace

Statistics show that 75 percent of people would prefer to have sex with the lights off—for multiple reasons, but one major fact is that people are uncomfortable with their bodies. While we are visual beings, intimacy is truly about the connection, the feeling, and the vibrations. Pun is most definitely intended when I say vibrations: vibrate higher!

Black lace gives you permission to indulge in sexual festivities freely. Love has no limits. No matter who you are, where you're from, the color of your skin, the amount of fat on your body, or the size of your stretch marks, everybody can use a nice orgasm. Black lace isn't only designed to camouflage stretch marks while trying to maintain a level of sexiness in the bedroom or in the back seat of your jeep if you're out and about; it is also about distracting the eyes from seeing the physical and allowing the body to feel the vibrations. After all, just like a mural is visual and music is audio, sex is the art that's vibrational. If you don't have eyes or ears. you can still feel your peak being reached.

8. Ride Your Own Wave

We are all earth mates. We are all supposed to use each other for help in one way or another. What we are not supposed to do is misuse one another. Learning how to tread the cataclysmic waters as much as we possibly can on our own will actually allow us to surf the waves as if it was a sport and will then cause our ships to sail more smoothly. Riding your own wave is a selfless act; in fact, it shows that you're unselfish because you don't want to misuse others by causing them to drown while trying to keep your head above water. Riding your own wave officially removes your crablike nature and allows you to be able to hold your own in your ships (relationships, friendships, fellowships).

9. Salubrious Vibrations

One of the best gifts we can offer others is good company. There's a whole world out here that we live in. People come from many different cultures, and peace is one of the things that we all can use, no matter where we're from. Be flexible! Allow yourself the ability to adapt and to bend without breaking.

There are over 7 billion people on this earth. Each one is different. Never assume that someone else is exactly like you. Though we will come across others with similarities, there will be differences as well. People won't want to give you what you want and need without having their wants and needs being met as well. Leave people better off than they were before they met you. Say something good. Share what makes you happy. Let them feel your passion. Make them want to hurry and go to sleep just so they can wake up in the morning with another shot at living a revised lifestyle.

We all have problems. We all have family members who get thrills when they see drama, so they create it intentionally for their own entertainment. Make the choice to be the one to bring healthy energy into the picture.

10. Paragon

I've learned that purpose comes before performance. Have you ever felt like you've been performing overtime and it serves or entertains others, but you're not being fulfilled? Your bills are being paid, but you're still confused, drained, or feeling used. Everyone has a purpose, and while many of us are still searching for ours, searching is a great goal in itself. We would add so much value to the world by becoming our best selves. Striving to be better and better every day would contribute to creating higher-frequency wave levels, which decrease the catastrophic energy that keeps us down and depressed.

Anxiety as well as many diseases come from the stress of others dumping their stuff into the universe. Believe it or not, we take on a lot of toxic energy daily without realizing it. If we all stayed driven in our own lanes and searched for our own destiny, as well as did the work that it takes to journey on, the love frequencies would rise. A paragon is a model or pattern of excellence or someone of exceptional merit. Nobody is perfect, but one of the rules of the game is to become the best person you can possibly be, no excuses. If we fall down, the goal would be to get back up and keep striving for greatness.

We are all different. We come from so many different backgrounds, cultures, races, religions, countries, sizes, sexualities, complexions, mindsets, and states of being, but working toward embracing differences and learning how to love through the differences is powerful. One thing we all have in common is the ability to dream, love, and let the music move us. Become the paragon that God created you to be. You don't need validation from others. Your existence is permission. It's okay to be great!